MW01128458

Jeanne F. Sanford
4084 Territorial Rd.
Benton Harbor, MI 49022

Love Never Ends

CONNIE MARTIN AND BARRY DUNDAS

Inspiring Voices®
A Service of Guideposts

Inspiring Voices books may be ordered through booksellers or by contacting:

Inspiring Voices
1663 Liberty Drive
Bloomington, IN 47403
www.inspiringvoices.com
1-(866) 697-5313

Cover photo of Northern Cardinal by Howard Cheek
Cover photo of Brandy Martin by Bill Roenne
Cover photo of Brookville Hotel by Diana Dundas

ISBN: 978-1-4624-0193-2 (sc)
ISBN: 978-1-4624-0192-5 (e)

Library of Congress Control Number: 2012941496

Printed in the United States of America

Inspiring Voices rev. date: 09/25/2012

$\mathcal{T}$able of Contents

Acknowledgements

I have been blessed by many people who have walked with me on my journey over the past 15 years. Each one has played an important role in my story. Some have moved both into and back out of my life in a short time, yet I know they were placed in my path for a reason. My story would not be the same without them. For each person I am incredibly grateful.

To my friend Audrey, thank you for the countless hours that you listened to me when I cried. Thank you for turning your life inside out to help a friend. I will never forget the sacrifice you made for Brandy and me.

To my friend Barry, thank you for being willing to listen, never judging me, and being willing to help me get this story on paper. We both know it would never have happened if God had not brought you to Salina, and our paths had not crossed. A special thank you to Diana, you supported Barry all the way, and helped by taking photos to bring the story to life. Your friendship has been a blessing to me.

Thank you to Michael and Kyla for reminding me that this is an important story to tell. You have often been the voice of reason when I questioned myself. I love you both as if you were my own children.

Thank you to my friend Jane for always being there for me. I know it was hard to believe at times, but you only loved me and never said the word crazy, not even once!

Thank you to Nedra, Carol, Kristin, Ted, and Mitch and to my good friend Trisha for taking time to read the story and help Barry and I get it right! You have been our best cheerleaders!!

And to my friend Kerry, I find it amusing that Brandy would find someone an entire world away and bring us together. You will always be an important part of this story.

To everyone who has encouraged us to write down this story, it could not have been done without your words of encouragement. Thank you to each of you.

Connie Martin

Foreword

I am a skeptic at heart. I am the last person in my family to believe a story is true. I think most things in this world have a logical explanation. I don't believe in most UFO stories, politicians who promise to lower taxes or sales that appear too good to be true. I do believe there are plenty of scam artists in the world whose only motivation is to separate people from their money. I even address questions of faith with a healthy dose of skepticism. That may surprise you coming from a pastor. It shouldn't; there are many pastors in the world just like me. Even as we read the Bible, we don't accept everything as fact. I have learned that there is difference between taking the Bible seriously and reading the Bible literally.

The big question I have asked myself many times is how did I get involved with this project? First, I am not an author. My writing experience has been limited to newsletter articles and seminary papers. Writing is neither my gift nor my passion in life. Second, this book is the kind of story that sends my skeptic radar into overload. Why in the world would I write a book about things that have no logical explanation? The simplest answer is that my friend Connie asked me to help her write her story and something inside me said yes. Something about her story is so compelling and so honest that I felt the desire to help her tell others. I could not say no.

Connie's biggest concern has been how people will respond to me when my name is on the book. The story we are telling is not mainstream United Methodist theology. There are many Christians who can be very critical of anything that is outside their experience in the church. Some pastors will not understand why I would take such a risk and connect myself to this book. I believe it is worth the risk because of the impact the story has had on my life.

The day Connie sat down in my office to share her story I could tell that she was being as honest as possible. She was not trying to convince me to believe something; she was telling me what she had experienced. I knew that she believed her experiences were real even if she was afraid that I did not. I saw no evidence that someone else was taking advantage of her grief or manipulating her for personal gain. Connie did not go seeking these experiences; they found her. The most important thing I saw in her story is how these amazing events helped bring healing to her spirit. My hope is that they can bring healing to lives of others who are hurting.

As a pastor, one of my concerns is how this story fits into my theology. It will be helpful for you to know that my theology is centered on grace, God's unconditional love for humanity. I believe there is nothing more important than love, loving God and loving neighbor. When I hear the messages from Brandy, they are consistent with my theology. She cannot stop talking about love. One night I was reading the thirteenth chapter of I Corinthians. It is sometimes called Paul's love chapter and therefore is read at about ninety percent of the weddings I perform. I often tell couples that it is a beautiful passage for their wedding, but Paul was not talking about marriage when he wrote it. Paul was talking about the most important thing in life – love. Without love we have missed the point; we are nothing. I realized that this chapter reflects Brandy's messages. She tells her mother the same thing and, ultimately, that love never ends. It is from the Apostle Paul that Connie and I found the title for our book.

This story has also impacted my ministry. One of the most important aspects of my role as a pastor is to minister to families through the death of a loved one. I have two responsibilities when I lead a funeral: to reflect on the person's life and to share some good news. I have discovered that through Connie's story I can now speak with confidence about my belief in life everlasting. Resurrection is central to the Gospel. Christians are resurrection people who live in hope that God can make all things new. Resurrection is no longer simply my hope but a reality I believe. God's love for us is so deep that even death cannot stop it.

This book is Connie and Brandy's story. It is a story of incredible pain and loss, but it is also a story about healing and love. My role has been to listen to Connie's voice and to put it on paper. As you read this story, my prayer is that you can open your mind to the possibilities of love and the promise that all of our lives have meaning and purpose in this world and the next.

Barry Dundas

Prologue

You Are to
Write a Book

$\mathcal{A}$ picture of the Virgin Mary hangs on the wall of the Brookville Hotel, the restaurant owned by my husband Mark and me. I purchased the print at a local antique store. Mark and I had just moved to town when I went exploring some of the downtown shops. Shopping is one of the things I do well, and I especially enjoy antique shops where I can find unique little treasures. I walked into the shop that day and there it sat, as if it were waiting for me. As soon as I saw the picture, I knew that I had to have it. I found the owner and asked if I could purchase the item. It had just arrived in her store, so she had not even put a price on it. I asked how much she wanted for the print, already knowing that I was going to buy it. The owner thought for a moment and suggested $100, a sum which I immediately agreed to pay. I could tell she was surprised by my quick response. I don't know if she thought she had asked too little or that I was an idiot for not making a counter offer. I didn't care; I didn't buy the picture because it was a bargain but because I knew I was supposed to have it.

Over the years, many of our customers have made comments about the picture as it is not the kind of artwork you see in most restaurants. I didn't know anything about the picture when I bought it except that it was the Virgin Mary. Customers who talk to me about the picture usually begin by asking where I found it. I tell them the story, and they say something like, "You know that is the *Assumption*?" I do now, but I knew nothing about the *Assumption* when I purchased the picture. In the picture I have, Mary is surrounded by children as she is taken up into heaven at the end of her life. Most people are surprised that I would put such an important piece of religious artwork on my wall and not know the story behind it. They are even more surprised when they discover I am not Catholic. Why would I display a picture of the Virgin Mary if I am not Catholic? My standard answer is that Mary is not Catholic either.

The main reason I put this picture on the restaurant wall is that it reminds me of my daughter Brandy. It hangs at the bottom of a staircase that leads to an upstairs apartment. When we were building the restaurant, Mark and I lived upstairs. After Brandy's death, I needed some reassurance that she was okay. Every morning when I walked downstairs into the real world, the first thing I would see was the picture of Mary on the wall. It brought me a sense of comfort and hope when my world often felt like chaos and hopelessness.

The picture of "The Assumption" that hangs in the Brookville Hotel

Fourteen years after Brandy's death, a doctor and his wife came into the restaurant for dinner, arriving just before our final seating of the evening. While waiting in the lobby, the woman noticed a family portrait on the wall. It was one of the last family photographs we had taken together. She asked if the young woman was our daughter and if she worked with us at the restaurant. As usual, I shared that she was our daughter, but she did not work with us. Remarking how beautiful Brandy was, the woman asked more questions. Typically I change the subject when that happens, but for some reason I told her that Brandy had died in 1995. Embarrassed, she offered her sympathy, and I assured her it was okay. Even more, I wanted her to know that I believed Brandy was okay.

Our last family portrait hangs in the hotel lobby

At that moment, her husband joined us and asked if I was the owner. He shared that they stop and eat at our restaurant every time they come through town and he always wanted to ask me about the picture of the *Assumption* on the wall. He had never seen a picture like that in a restaurant. I told him the story of how the picture made it to that spot on the wall and how it brought me comfort after my daughter's death. I assured both of them again of my confidence that Brandy was okay and that I believed she was still active in my life. I don't know why I was sharing such personal information with a couple I had just met. Sometimes I just want to tell myself to shut up! The man listened carefully and then said, "You are a very faithful Catholic." I looked at him and said, "You won't believe this, but I'm not Catholic at all; I'm Methodist!"

By this time it was too late to turn back. I opened up and started telling all I had experienced since Brandy died. There is always a point after I start sharing my story when I am sure the listener is going to think, "This lady is simply nuts." Either they keep listening to see just how crazy I am or decide that what I have experienced is real. So we stood in the lobby of the restaurant for over an hour and talked. All the customers had left, and even Mark had gone home to grill some hamburgers. Finally Mark came back to the restaurant, burgers in hand, wondering what had happened to me.

It is hard to explain our conversation that night. There are just some people you meet in life who you can talk to as if you have known them forever. As we shared our stories, something spiritual was happening. The more we talked, the more energy I felt in the room, and the tears begin to flow. The doctor paused for a moment, then said, "You need to write this down. You are supposed to tell this story." It was as if something had changed about him, almost as if he were not the one telling me this information. He continued, "You will bring many to her Son through your sorrows." I looked at him, speechless. Something about that statement was piercing my own heart. The atmosphere in the room was surreal, as if I was receiving a message from above. The doctor had my attention.

I have known for years that I am supposed to tell my story, but I have always had a truckload of excuses. Finally I unloaded my entire list on my new friends, "I know I need to write it down, but I can't do it now. I don't have the time. My father is very sick and I have to take care of him. We don't have enough help at the restaurant so I have to work. I am so busy that I don't even have time to polish my nails. Besides," and this was my biggest excuse of all, "I can't write."

His wife looked at me and said, "People would rather read a book by someone who can't write but has something to say than a book by someone who is a great writer but has nothing to say." I appreciated her words of encouragement and her interest in my story.

I made more excuses about my lack of literary skills, how I had tried writing before but it just didn't work. If this book were ever going to be written, I was going to need help. The doctor stopped for a moment and looked at me. He said, "You already know who is going to help write this book, don't you?" Once again I was stunned; how could he have known that? A year earlier I had received an e-mail from my pastor. It was a just a silly story but after reading the first few sentences I knew its author. As I was reading, a voice in my head said clearly, "He can tell the story." The problem is that he didn't know the story. I had not told him yet. I wanted a few people in my life who thought I was normal. How was I going to convince him to write the story? When I finally had the courage to share with him the things that had happened to me and tell him that I believed he was supposed to write it, his response surprised even me. He said, "My wife is always asking me when I am going to write my first book."

Even if I already knew who could write my story, I still did not have any free time in my life. For the last three years I had been the primary caregiver for my father. He lived in an assisted care facility 25 miles away. Most of my expendable time was consumed with taking care of his needs.

The Tuesday after my conversation with the couple in the restaurant I received a call early in the morning; Daddy was gone. It was a very peaceful and quick death. I was heartbroken that my father had died, but I also had a feeling of relief. My father had been so lonely and sad since Mom died three years earlier. In his final years he was not the same man that I had known. He hurt all the time, he was tired and he struggled to remember the simplest things. It is difficult to watch someone you love slowly slip away. When death finally comes, there is an odd mixture of sadness and relief. As I stood in the shower that morning I realized, "Now I don't have an excuse, it is time to tell my story." A few weeks later I sat down with my pastor and we began to write this book.

Chapter 1

The Worst Day
of My Life

The best way I can describe our only daughter, Brandy, is to say that living, she was an old soul with a wisdom and compassion often well beyond her years. She was easy-going with a great sense of humor. She had many friends, but was not always interested in the same things. She often found herself dancing to her own beat while her friends engaged in other activities.

Our relationship was typical of most mothers who have only one child. I admit that I could be overprotective and I often bought her more things than she really needed. It is hard not to spoil a child who has no brothers and sisters. There is no one to compete with for attention or possessions. Mark and I worked hard to give Brandy a typical childhood, but she had many advantages as an only child.

When Brandy was younger, we did everything together. As an only child, she spent much of her time in my world, surrounded by adults. As I look back, I believe that because of these experiences, she grew up faster than other children with a maturity beyond her years. We still had our share of conflicts just like every mother and teenage daughter. I am the first to admit that our relationship was far from perfect, but my love for her was deeper than any I have ever experienced with another human being.

When Brandy was a senior in high school, she started getting one sore throat after another. She had always suffered with allergies, but this was something new. She had never experienced this much trouble with her health. Brandy was an excellent student, taking college prep courses, but missing school four days at a time was not helping her studies. She would go on antibiotics for ten to twelve days, and then her illness would begin again. After four rounds of treatments, it was time to see an ear, nose and throat specialist. He quickly decided that her tonsils needed to come out.

As I look back, I wonder if I should have asked more questions, but everything appeared to be routine. Tonsillectomies are performed every day on children and adults. There was no reason to suspect this would be any different. She was scheduled for outpatient surgery at a time that was convenient for our busy schedules. She would go in, have the tonsils removed, come home, eat a little ice cream and be back in school before we knew it. Why would we expect anything else?

The first sign that something was not right was the afternoon after the surgery. Brandy was having trouble swallowing so the doctor decided to keep her in the hospital overnight. His explanation was the tonsils had been really big, and therefore she was experiencing extra swelling. It was nothing for us to be concerned about. I stayed with her that night, and it was miserable. Brandy couldn't sleep because of the pain and consistent nausea. Medication given to help her sleep was not successful. She kept complaining about pain in her neck, and she was unable to turn her head.

The day after surgery was no better. Brandy still could not swallow and the pain was not going away. Because she could not speak, the only way for her to communicate with us was by writing. It was decided that she should spend a second night in the hospital. I was determined to stay with her, but she wrote me a note: "Mom, go home, you look like crap! I will be fine." I was convinced that she was right, so I did go home to get some much needed rest.

The following morning Brandy was released from the hospital. She was still having trouble swallowing and her neck mobility was not getting any better. Everything was still very painful, but she was ready to be out. She had things to do and was determined not to let a little sore throat get in the way. She had a date the following Saturday that would not be possible if she were lying in a hospital bed. By the fourth night after surgery, Brandy was not eating or drinking well, and Mark and I were concerned. We explained to her that if she was unable to drink any fluids, we would need to go back to the hospital.

That night I was exhausted and went to bed early hoping that Brandy would feel better in the morning. Mark stayed up with her, encouraging her to drink more fluids and to try and eat a little food. I fell into a deep sleep and hardly noticed when Mark finally came to bed.

The next thing I remember was the light coming on in my room. I looked at the clock, and it was a little before four a.m. Brandy had walked into our room, turned on the light and was standing near the sink in the bathroom. She never said a word; she just looked at me and I could see the fear in her eyes. It was a mixture of terror and pleading for help. I noticed a little blood coming out of her nose. I cried out, "Oh my God, she is bleeding." Mark and I both jumped out of bed and he yelled, "Call 911!"

As I dialed the phone next to our bed, Mark ran to Brandy. She stepped away from the sink toward him and fell into his arms. I have played that moment in my head many times because it was so surreal. He didn't just catch her as she was falling to the floor; it was as if someone picked her up and laid her in his arms. She collapsed right there and the weight of her body took him to his knees. When he opened her mouth to administer CPR, blood began to pour out over both Mark and Brandy.

The people who answer 911 calls are trained to be calm in a crisis, but I was anything but calm on the phone. I started screaming, "My daughter, she's bleeding!" As the operator started asking me the series of questions that I am sure she was trained to recite, I could not convey the urgency of the situation I was frantic as I yelled, "You don't understand, she is bleeding! You have to hurry!" Calmly the operator assured me that help was on the way.

I had never been in a situation like this before in my life. The panic and anxiety that rushed through my being resembled the scene in front of me. Everything felt like it was moving in fast motion and slow motion at the same time. To this day, my memory of those first few moments still feel like an eternity, when in reality I know they only lasted a few minutes.

Our house was part of a new subdivision and I was scared that the ambulance would have trouble finding us, so I grabbed a robe and went outside to wave them down. It was a cold night and even though I could hear the siren in the distance, it seemed like hours for the first fire truck to arrive. When the paramedic got out of his vehicle, I pleaded for him to hurry. I understand that these professionals are trained not to panic, but again it seemed as if I could not explain the urgency of the situation.

As the paramedic walked into the house I was frantic. I remained outside on the street feeling helpless. My whole world was collapsing around me. Then, strangely an incredible peace washed over me and I knew at that moment Brandy was gone. No one had to tell me, I just knew it in the core of my being; my daughter had left this world. I couldn't move. I just stood in my front yard as if I were paralyzed. By this time, lights were coming on in our neighbors' houses as they were waking up from the sound of sirens. One of my concerned neighbors walked over to me and I said to her, "She's gone." She responded, "You don't know that," but she was wrong; I did know it. My neighbor grabbed a blanket and put it around me. I was still just in my robe standing outside in forty-degree weather. She walked into the house to see what was happening and returned to tell me the medics were doing everything they could. It didn't matter; I already knew my only daughter, the love of my life, was dead.

I couldn't go back into the house; it was too painful. Eventually the attendants wheeled Brandy out on a stretcher. I could see her long blond hair falling over the sides. Mark, covered in blood, walked beside her. He rode with her in the ambulance to the hospital. I couldn't do it, so a police officer gave me a ride. I am sure I was in shock, but I was remarkably calm. It felt as if I were watching the whole event rather than participating in it. In the police car I asked if I could use the phone. I called my mom and said, "I am sorry to bother you, but Brandy is dead. She bled to death; we are on our way to the hospital." I cannot imagine what my mom must have thought at that moment, but all she replied was, "We are on our way."

When we arrived at the hospital, Mark was with Brandy, but I couldn't go in. I remained in the waiting room with my parents. The nurse finally came out to give me the news I already knew. Brandy was dead. She had died from a ruptured aneurysm in her neck. The nurse did not tell us at the time, but later we discovered that during the tonsillectomy the surgeon had nicked her carotid artery. That is why she was having the neck pain and extra swelling. When the aneurysm ruptured, she lost so much blood that she died almost instantly. The nurse asked if I would like to go in and say goodbye. I couldn't go in to see her, so my father sat with me while my mother went in for both of us.

I didn't see Brandy's body until the visitation at the funeral home. My whole being simply shut down and I could not function. I truly depended on my friends for the next few days. I didn't want to go to the funeral home, but my friends convinced me I had to. The only thing I remember is that my legs felt like two pieces of lead. It took every ounce of energy I had just to move them.

The sanctuary of our church holds only about 300 people. I don't know how many attended Brandy's funeral, but I believe it was well over 1000. Not only was the sanctuary packed, the entire building was filled to capacity. The hallways were lined with chairs and Sunday school rooms had TV's to air a live feed of the service. The service lasted about an hour, but it took us another two hours to greet and thank everyone who had come to support our family. We were amazed and overwhelmed by the outpouring of love.

The last person to greet us was the paramedic who had arrived at the house. A young man in his twenties, he was dressed in uniform, his hat under his arm. He was in tears as he apologized for not running into the house and for not being able to do more. He said, "I was not prepared for what I saw that night; it was not what I expected." I thanked him for coming to the service and for having the courage to talk to us. How could he have been prepared for that night? How could any of us have been prepared for that experience or for what I was going to have to face in the days to come?

Chapter 2

I Don't Want to Live

After Brandy's death, my whole life went numb. Unless you have experienced the death of a child, you cannot understand the depth of pain a human being can feel. Mark and I asked all the "what if" questions. What if we had pushed the doctors harder on why she could not swallow? What if we had taken her back to the hospital that night? What if we had not waited for the ambulance but had taken her to the hospital immediately? What if we had never elected for the surgery in the first place? We spent a lot of time blaming ourselves, but it only made the pain worse.

Losing my only child was the most helpless feeling in the world. What made it worse is that everyone knew what had happened. When I went out into the community, everyone wanted to come up and tell me how sorry they felt. They would ask, "How are you doing?" I wanted to respond, "How do you think I am doing! My whole life has just come crashing down around me! I guess, considering the circumstances, I am doing just dandy!"

Obviously I wasn't doing just dandy. What I wanted to do was run away from everything. I wanted to move to a little house where nobody knew my story, where there was no telephone and I wouldn't have to talk to anyone. I wanted to go where I didn't have to put on a happy face. I didn't want to see any more people, ever, not even Mark.

The thought that scared me the most is that I could live another forty years with this pain. I could not fathom hurting that bad for that long. I just could not do it. After a couple of weeks I hit my breaking point. I could not keep it together any longer. I called one of my doctors and told him I was having trouble sleeping. I asked if he could write me a prescription to help me get some rest. My plan was to pick up the prescription, drive to a secluded place where no one would find me for hours, even days, and quietly make the pain stop.

As I walked into the garage to get into my car, the phone rang. I almost did not answer it. What difference did it make? I had a plan and answering the phone was just going to delay the process. For some unknown reason I picked up the phone and it was my friend Audrey.[1] Audrey had been one of my closest friends for years. She had moved out of state but had flown back to spend a few days with me after Brandy's death. She had returned home from her visit, so I was not surprised to hear her voice.

Audrey asked, "Are you having a tough day?"

---

[1] Some names have been changed in the story including Audrey's

In my most sarcastic tone I responded, "No, it is an absolutely great day!"

"Are you busy?" she asked.

"Not really," I said. "I was just getting ready to leave and run a few errands." It was not really a lie. I had to go to the pharmacy to get my prescription before I carried out my plan.

For a moment there was silence on the phone. Then Audrey blurted out, "She wants you to know that the pills are not the answer!" It was like someone hit me in the stomach. You know that feeling when you get caught in a lie? Your heart starts to race and you get that funny feeling that everyone can see right through you.

I paused for what seemed like a long time. Then I finally said, "I don't know what you're talking about."

"Yes, you do, and she wants you to know that the pills are not the answer," Audrey pleaded. "She needs you to know that she is okay and that she has never left your side. Oh, Connie, it is okay if you don't believe me, but Brandy needs you to know she is okay. She looks so beautiful; her hair is flowing in the wind."

"Don't mess with me, Audrey!" I said emphatically.

"I am not messing with you," she said. "She just needs you to understand this one thing. She is okay and she has never left your side."

I don't remember much more of that conversation, but I know I did not go to the pharmacy. I don't think I believed Audrey at that moment, but something kept me from following through with my plan. Maybe I was in shock or maybe I was still in too much pain to think straight. I didn't even know what questions to ask. Had my good friend Audrey really heard from my dead daughter? Was that even possible?

Weeks later I asked Audrey about that day. She told me she had been on her hands and knees scrubbing her kitchen floor when suddenly there was something in the room with her. It was Brandy, there in her kitchen, glowing like the sun. Although she was startled, she was not frightened because there was such a peace in the room. Brandy said to her, "Don't be afraid. You have to help my mom. She has to know that I am okay."

Audrey didn't say anything for a minute. When she could finally respond, she doesn't know if she spoke out loud or just thought. She does remember that she didn't have to speak; there was just an understanding between them. The first thing Audrey communicated was, "Why don't you tell her yourself?"

Brandy had a simple answer, "I have tried, but she can't hear me. Mom is so sad and angry that she can't hear me. She needs to know that I love her and that I will always be with her. You need to hurry! She is in trouble!"

Audrey was still stunned, thinking, "How do you call your friend who is grieving the loss of her only child and tell her that her daughter has come to visit you? She will think I am crazy and she might be so hurt that I will lose a wonderful friendship." She asked Brandy, "Am I just supposed to pick up the phone and call her?"

"Yes, because that is what friends do," she replied. I asked Audrey how she had found the courage to call me that day and literally save my life. She said that it was the absolute love and concern she felt from Brandy. Brandy knew I was in trouble and had to get to me somehow.

Early the next morning I received another call from Audrey. She couldn't talk yet because she was busy with her children, but she needed to make sure I would be home later that morning so she could call me back. She promised as soon as she got her kids off to school that I would receive another call from her. I was surprised by the urgency in her voice so I said sarcastically, "What's the rush; did you talk to Brandy again?" She responded with a quick yes and hung up the phone.

Later that morning Audrey called me back. She shared that Brandy had visited her again with a new message, "Mother will hear me in the music." You have to understand that Audrey knows little about music, especially pop music. About the only music she listens to is Pavarotti. Brandy told her that she needed to go the music store and buy two CDs. The first was Elton John's *Made in England* and the second was a compilation of Grammy Award winning songs from that year. Both CD's had just been released, and she needed to get them to me.

Audrey found them at the music store, packaged them up so she could mail them the next day, but that morning Audrey woke up early with another message from Brandy. Apparently, she was concerned that I still did not have the CD's; why was it taking so long? Audrey tried to explain that they were ready to be mailed, but that was not fast enough for Brandy. Audrey would have to call me and tell me to buy the CDs. That is when she made the first call of the morning. The CD of Grammy Award-winning music was songs that Brandy enjoyed and would remind me of her, but there was a particular song on the Elton John CD that she needed me to hear. It was a song called "House."

I drove to Target and found both CDs. I also picked up a six pack of beer and a pack of cigarettes and drove to the lake to listen to the music. The irony is that I don't often drink beer and I hate cigarette smoke. I was still not in a good place and I was looking to numb the pain. In my twisted logic, I thought if I started smoking cigarettes, I would die sooner. I know that doesn't make sense, but nothing in my life was making much sense. My friend, Martha, shared with me later that if I really wanted to kill myself with cigarettes I would have to inhale. I probably had the shortest smoking habit in history.

I came home that day sick to my stomach from the beer and cigarettes but beginning a new relationship with Brandy through music. As I listened to the words of Elton John's song "House," I began to weep. Our house was the last place I had seen Brandy alive. Her room still had all of her belongings. Some days I would go up to her closet just to hold her clothes because I could still smell her on them. Here are the words of the song.

This is my house
This is where I live
That is the winter
Those are the trees
I can hear them breathe
This is my bed
This is where I sleep
That was the dark
Those are my dreams
They belong to me
This is my floor

This is where I lie
This is a square room
That was a bright light
These are not my eyes
What is my soul
Where is my tired heart
That is the question
Where is the answer
Inside my house
And I sit by the window
And I wish I was rain
I want to fall from the sky
I want to get wet all over again
'Cause this is my house
It belongs to me
Inside my head
It's all that's left
This is my house
This is my bed
This is where I sleep
That was the dark
Those are my dreams
They belong to me
This is my house[2]

[2] **House** Words and Music by Elton John and Bernie Taupin
Copyright ©1995 WRETCHED MUSIC
All Rights Controlled and Administered by UNIVERSAL –
POLYGRAM INTERNATIONAL PUBLISHING, INC.
All rights reserved. Used by permission
Reprinted by permission of Hal Leonard Corporation

One line that caught my attention was "These are not my eyes." There is not another line like it in the song. The other similar phrases claim possession of the object: "This is my house. This is my bed. These are my dreams. This is my floor etc . . . ." Why the line, "These are not my eyes"? Did Elton John make a mistake when writing the lyrics?

When Brandy died, we wanted to donate her organs so that someone else might receive life. However, because she had lost so much blood so rapidly, most of her organs were too damaged to use. The only part of her that was given away, that now belonged to someone else, were her eyes. For the average listener, the line is hardly noticeable. For me it may have been the moment I started to believe.

That night Audrey called me back to see how I was doing. I told her about the song and what I had heard. Audrey had one more message. "Brandy wants you to know that the beer and the cigarettes are not the answer either!"

Chapter 3

Am I Going Crazy?

*B*efore Brandy died, I had not spent much time thinking about death or what is on the other side of this life. Such thoughts scared me. Even when my parents bought their headstones and six plots in a little country cemetery outside of town, I could not face death. They wanted to sit down and talk about plans for their funerals, and I simply refused. It wasn't that I had not heard the stories from the Bible. I was a Christian who grew up in the church. I knew the story of resurrection and life after death. I always thought "what a great story," but I always added, "if it is true." Then I was brought to my knees by Brandy's death and confronted with the questions I did not want to face.

Brandy was buried in that little cemetery in one of the plots owned by my parents. Many days I would feel this uncontrollable pull to the cemetery. When it hit, I could not get there fast enough. Overcome with grief, all I could think about was getting to the cemetery. We had left our daughter there, and now she was all alone. I would sit by her grave for hours and just cry and cry. What I didn't understand is that it wasn't Brandy who was all alone, it was me.

At this time, Audrey became my lifeline. I didn't know if I believed her yet, but it was all I had to hold on to. Both of us questioned whether we could trust what we were experiencing or if we were slowly losing our minds. We would spend hours on the phone. These were the days before unlimited long distance calling and I was racking up outrageous phone bills. I could not get enough. I had so many questions. Sometimes she would give me immediate responses and other times she would simply say, "I don't know." Often she would call back the next day and share something Brandy wanted me to understand. She did not always have the words. She would say, "I don't know if the English language has the words to express the absolute love and joy she is experiencing."

One question I had is how did Brandy communicate with her? Did she see her? What did she look like? Did she use words? Where was she? Audrey answered the questions the best she could. She told me one day, "Brandy wants you to know that she is not at the cemetery. The only time she is there is when you go out there. You can keep going if it gives you comfort, but don't go out of guilt that you left her there. She is with you." She added, "And Brandy says quit leaving flowers out there, put them on the piano where we can both enjoy them!"

One evening I received a call from Audrey. She was very excited and told me to turn on *Larry King Live*; she would call me back when the show was over. Larry's guest that night was John Edward, a man of whom I had never heard. He was talking about his experience of communicating with people who had crossed over. After the broadcast, Audrey called back and said, "That's it! That's what happens to me. I knew exactly what he was talking about. If I could crawl into his skin I would have said the exact same things." Communication with a deceased person was a totally new experience for Audrey. She needed to know she was not alone in experiencing such a phenomenon.

Even with these communications through Audrey, neither Mark nor I was doing well. I would not have been surprised to receive a phone call saying his truck had been found at the bottom of a lake. People were trying to be nice, but often they made such insensitive comments such as "If you had other children this would be easier," or "You are still young enough that you could adopt children." I know these remarks were said out of love, but others didn't understand the pain we were feeling. Nothing was going to replace Brandy.

Each day I would force myself to get up and get dressed. I would drive to Target to buy something like toilet paper or toothpaste. Then I would go home. That was the most I could accomplish on most days. There was nothing special about the Target store except it was new in town and Brandy had been excited that we were getting a Target. By going there I was holding on to one more connection to my daughter, trying to keep myself sane.

Some good friends were worried enough about Mark and me that they made us an appointment with a grief counselor in Kansas City. They even drove us down to make sure we would get there. On the way I asked if I should tell the counselor about the messages through Audrey. My friends were not sure it would be a good idea. Not everyone was going to believe me.

The counselor was a stereotypical psychiatrist – a tall, thin woman in a grey suit with her hair in a bun – and I soon realized that I didn't have to worry about spilling the beans on my messages from Brandy. All Mark and I did that first visit was sit in her office and cry. She decided that she needed to see us separately if she was ever going to make any progress. We made arrangements for another appointment.

On our second visit I began to feel comfortable talking with her. I wanted to believe that what I was experiencing from Audrey was real, but I questioned my own sanity. I finally asked her, "Do you think it is possible to communicate with loved ones who have passed."

"Absolutely," she responded. "Has that happened?"

My first thought was, "This is a trick question. She answered too quickly. I think she is setting me up so that she can admit me into the mental ward of the hospital. I wasn't going to be caught that easily so I said, "Maybe, I don't know."

She invited me to tell her the story. I pondered my options for a moment. What did I have to lose? If I was ever going to receive help then I had to be honest. Once I made the decision and started talking to her, I could not stop. Everything came pouring out. I told her about the first call, the songs, the questions and all the long distance phone calls with my friend Audrey. When I finally stopped, she looked at me and said, "Connie, I have been doing this for over 40 years and I have heard the same stories over and over again. There has to be some truth to them." She went on to share some of the things that other people had told her. "I don't think everyone could be hallucinating the same kind of experiences. Besides, they always bring such peace and understanding, that they are even therapeutic."

The psychiatrist had listened to these stories many times, but it was her own experience that finally convinced her to take them seriously. One of the founding doctors at her clinic had become terminally ill. He was very well-liked and respected by the staff, and they took turns sitting with him at the hospital. The doctor was afraid of dying, and whenever my counselor would visit him, he would ask her to sing. She would sing some old hymn, and then he would ask, "Tell me again what you think happens when we die."

"I think when God calls you, God will be there waiting," she would say. "Everyone you have ever loved will be there waiting. It will be like simply opening a door and going through."

Every time she would go to visit, they would share the same routine. She would sing some old hymns and then he would ask her the same question, "Tell me again what you think happens when we die." Once again she would share with him what she believed to be true.

My counselor was not with her friend and mentor when he died. She was on a trip to Paris when she received word of his passing. That night she had a strange dream. All of a sudden she was out of her body looking at herself from above the bed. She noted that she looked horrible sleeping with her mouth wide open. Then she was no longer in the room but with the doctor. He was much younger; he looked as if he were in his thirties. There he stood with his arm around his brothers and his family was surrounding him. Everyone was smiling, and he said to her, "You were right." The next thing she knew she was being forced back into her body which felt like a lump of clay. She remarked how freeing it had been to be outside of her body. Then she woke up.

I left her office that day feeling not quite so alone in the world. If this was all just imagined in my head and I was going insane, I was definitely not alone.

Chapter 4

Visitor in the Night

I wasn't sure if Mark really believed any of the things that were happening to me or the messages that were coming from Audrey. We were not communicating very well. Both of us were hurting badly; often that meant taking our pain out on each other. There is a reason that couples who lose a child often end up divorced. I wondered if Mark was going along with my stories about Brandy just to keep the peace or so he wouldn't burst my bubble. I was still having trouble believing it was true and if he verbally questioned the story, I might just go over the edge.

It didn't help that the rest of my family had very little to give. A month before Brandy died, my younger sister, Kristie, had died from a bout with the flu, leaving behind her husband

and a five-year-old daughter. Kristie had been diagnosed with lupus at the age of 13. Most people never knew the health issues she battled because she did not dwell on them. However her immune system was so poor that little things like the flu were life-threatening. The day before she was taken to the hospital, I had called asking if she needed anything like medicine or 7-Up but she refused. She was just tired and was going to bed.

The next morning, Kristie collapsed in her hallway and was rushed to the hospital. She remained in a coma for ten days until we finally removed life-support. My father never forgave himself for not taking Kristie to the hospital sooner. Like all parents who have lost a child, he constantly played the what-if game. When Brandy died a month later, it was a double punch to the gut for our family. Within thirty days, my parents had buried both a daughter and a granddaughter, and I had lost a sister and a child. How could we possibly be there for one another when we were all so broken?

Audrey would come to visit and say things like "Can't you feel her? She is still present here with you." I know she was trying to give me comfort, but as hard as I tried, I couldn't feel her. All I could feel was the pain and the emptiness. The only time I felt connected to my daughter was in the music. Brandy was still telling Audrey to give me songs that had messages from her. When I listened to the songs, the tears would flow, and for a moment I would feel close to her once again.

Most of the time Audrey would give me songs I had never heard before and I was certain she had never heard either. The words would do more than bring me comfort; as I would listen, they would speak to my soul. One of the first songs she shared with me was *Love Has a Hold on Me* by Amy Grant. Here are some of the words.

I have found a perfect mystery
Love has a hold on me
Long before my life had come to be
Love had a hold on me

Where do I come from
What does life mean
Is it not to know the one who made me

As I'm looking down the road ahead
Love has a hold on me
Someday when I breathe my dying breath
Love has a hold on me

Where will I go
When this life is through
Back into the light that made me and you

Love has a hold on me
Something opened up my eyes to see
Love has a hold on me

> *I don't have answers to all the questions*
> *Running inside of my mind*
> *But I can't help believe that*
> *Understanding comes in time*[3]

Music seemed a natural way for Brandy to communicate. It was a big part of our life together. I grew up in a family that gathered regularly around the piano to sing together. They are some of my best memories, full of joy and laughter. Brandy inherited my love for music and now it was one of the few ways I could remain close to her.

Sometimes a song would simply start playing on the radio, and I knew Brandy was with me. A few weeks after Brandy died, I was driving to Oklahoma and the song *Shattered* by Linda Ronstadt began to play. It was as if Brandy were sitting in the car with me. I was so shaken that I had to pull over on the side of the road. The words said exactly what I was feeling.

---

[3]   **Love Has A Hold On Me** Words and Music by Amy Grant and Keith Thomas
Copyright ©1994 Age to Age Music, Inc. (ASCAP) / Riverstone Music (ASCAP) (both admin by The Loving Company), Sony/ATV Music Publishing LLC, Dimensional Music Of 1091, Reunion Music.
All rights on behalf of Sony/ATV Music Publishing LLC administered by Sony/ATV Music Publishing LLC, 8 Music Square West, Nashville, TN 37203.
Worldwide Rights for Dimensional Music of 1091 Administered by Cherry Lane Music Publishing Company, Inc.
International Copyright secured All rights reserved. *Reprinted by permission of Cherry Lane Music Company*

Shattered
Like a windowpane
Broken by a stone
Each tiny piece of me lies alone

And scattered
Far beyond repair
All my shiny dreams
Just lying there

I'm broken, but I'm laughing
It's the sound of falling glass
I hope that you won't mind if I should cry,
In public, while I wait for this to pass

'Cause sweet darling I'm shattered
Into fragments cold and gray
Sweep the pieces all away
Then no one will ever know how much it mattered
Something deep inside of me
Shattered[4]

---

[4] **Shattered** Words and Music by Jimmy Webb
Copyright ©1982 WHITE OAKS SONGS
All Rights Controlled and Administered by UNIVERSAL –
POLYGRAM INTERNATIONAL PUBLISHING, INC.
All rights reserved. Used by permission
Reprinted by permission of Hal Leonard Corporation

Mark and I both felt shattered by the loss of our daughter. Neither of us could sleep well. At night one of us would lie in the bed while the other roamed the house. Then the other would come to bed while the one who had been trying to sleep would get up and roam. Sometimes we would both roam and other times one of us would lie down on the couch to keep from waking the other. Sleep was precious, and when it came we tried not to disturb it.

One night I took something to help me sleep. When I woke that morning, I noticed that Mark was not in bed. Of course this was not unusual for our night time pattern. Even if we both slept in the bed, Mark usually got up earlier than I did. I tried to stay in bed as long as possible to avoid facing the day. What was unusual is how I found him that morning. Mark was fully dressed, sitting on the couch, almost in a daze.

Mark had woken up in the night hurting from a kidney stone that needed to pass. He has suffered from kidney stones for years, so he knew exactly what caused his pain. He knew he needed to go to the hospital, but did not want to wake me if I was truly getting some much-needed rest. He quietly got dressed so that he could drive himself to the hospital. He understood that he had a little time before the pain would make it impossible to drive, but Mark never made it to the hospital.

When I found him fully dressed that morning sitting on the couch, I asked, "What are you doing?"

His reply was simply, "She was here."

"Who was here?" I said.

"Brandy."

Of course, I wanted every detail about what he had experienced in the early hours of that morning. I still didn't know about the kidney stone or his plans to go to the hospital. Honestly, I probably would not have cared; I was just hungry for information. I have asked him to tell me the story many times since, and it never changes. Each time it is as if he is there all over again.

When Mark decided that he needed to go to the hospital, he had gotten up and quietly dressed. He sat down on the couch to put on his socks and shoes, and then she was there, sitting beside him. I asked if he saw her and he said yes, for just a moment, but it was more of a presence. She didn't say things like, "Don't worry about me, I'm okay" or "I am here with you always." Instead she said, "Daddy, you need to drink." Then she sat and patted his leg. He shared with me that he could actually feel her hand softly touching his leg.

Mark got up, went to the kitchen and drank a big glass of water. Thirty minutes later he passed the stone without ever going to the hospital. He returned to the couch which is where I found him that morning. I believe he didn't want to leave the spot where he had felt so close to his daughter.

That night changed things for Mark and me. It didn't stop the hurting or completely heal our relationship, but it did begin to bring us back together. It didn't stop us from questioning what was happening in our lives or keep us from asking why, but I did stop worrying if Mark thought I was imagining everything. These were no longer just the experiences of a mother blinded by grief who would look for anything to relieve her pain. Now these were experiences we could share as a husband and wife, walking our journey together again.

Chapter 5

Don't Be Afraid to Sing

$\mathcal{I}$ do not look forward to the holidays. Thanksgiving and Christmas are the worst because we close the restaurant. Those are days set aside to spend with family. Other holidays like Mother's Day and Father's Day are not as bad for us because we are busy at the restaurant. I did not know how I was going to face my first Christmas after Brandy's death.

I had almost completely stopped working at the restaurant. So many people who came in knew our story and wanted to stop and give me sympathy. It was too much to face every day so I didn't. A good friend, Jane, who played the organ at my church and taught at a school in a low income neighborhood, invited me to be her teacher aide. It was a perfect opportunity because it gave me a reason to get out of bed. These children didn't know the turmoil in my life, and I didn't have to pretend to be okay. Three days a week I would go in to create bulletin boards, grade papers or do whatever my friend needed. It was a wonderful distraction

We spent a lot of time talking about what had happened in my life since Brandy died. I needed someone to tell me I wasn't going crazy, that I wasn't making this all up in my head. Jane listened without a hint of judgment and said, "I don't think it is crazy at all. Why are you having such a hard time with it? What's it going to take for you to believe?" I didn't know what it was going to take, but her validation and friendship were essential.

Audrey and I were still talking on the phone almost daily. One morning she called and asked if I had a nativity. It was an odd question even if it was getting close to Christmas. I asked her to repeat the question.

"Do you have a nativity set?" she asked.

"I don't."

"Have you ever had one?"

"No, why are you asking this?"

"I was looking through the Neiman Marcus Christmas catalog and the first six pages are all nativity sets. Brandy keeps saying 'Get that one for my mother.' I try to ignore her but she keeps bringing it up. She wants you to have a nativity set because she says 'It is the most important story ever told.'" Audrey used to say that when Brandy wanted something she was very persistent, like an annoying little gnat that would not go away. I told her she didn't need to buy a nativity, but it was too late. She had already purchased it. It is a very simple nativity with only five small pieces: Mary, Joseph, an angel, the manger and the baby Jesus. It didn't even have a stable. Brandy said not to worry, "My daddy will build one." She was right.

Decorating the house for Christmas had always been one of the highlights of the season. Even with the new nativity set I was having a hard time getting into the Christmas spirit. This year I had no desire to put up any decorations. Audrey called with another message, "She wants you to put up a tree. She says to make it an angel tree and she will be dancing among the branches." I argued that I just couldn't do it this year, it was too painful, but Audrey was clear that Brandy really wanted an angel tree.

If that is what Brandy wanted, then she was going to get her angel tree. I went out and bought every angel decoration I could find. We put the tree up in the living room and covered it in angels and lights. It was a painful process, but it did begin to feel a bit more like Christmas. A few weeks later we received a letter from Audrey.

Dear Connie and Mark,

This letter has taken some time for me to write, it has been a project for over a month. I found it hard to write because I didn't want to cause you more pain in this beautiful season. I have tried to get out all the feelings she has expressed but when I put it onto paper it does not begin to truly tell you her feelings. I become so sad, I don't want to continue and then her expression of joy and love for both of you fills me beyond words. It is so difficult. I am only one person living here on this earth trying to tell you how this beautiful little angel feels and I can't come near to what it really is. I have become frustrated, torn up the papers and then we start again. I wish I could bring joy and love back to you both but I guess I can only attempt to try. If you can imagine the most beautiful feeling we have within ourselves, one of total peace and love. That is what she is trying to express. Her feelings are only of sadness for how you feel. She is in total heaven. I will never understand how all of this happens. I complain a lot of why I have been given this to do, it is difficult to understand and frustrating because our language doesn't have words so it then moves into feelings. I could write pages more but it still wouldn't cover it all. She loves you beyond words and there is nothing that she can do to fill the hole in your hearts. She is always with you and will be waiting until you are all together again.

Love,
Audrey

P.S. She really wants you to sing – I'm sorry, she keeps bringing it up, and if you don't sing – well you tell her, she hears you.

I knew exactly what she was asking. I had sung solos in the church choir for years. One of Brandy's favorite songs was an arrangement of *Silent Night*. She had heard it many times during choir rehearsals and in worship, but I had not sung a solo since her death. The thought of singing one of her favorite pieces was more than I could fathom. I would never be able to keep it together during the song.

I went to work at the school the next day and told my friend about the letter. I shared that I had a feeling Brandy wanted me to sing *Silent Night* this Christmas. Without hesitation she said, "Well, you have to sing it! It would be perfect for Christmas Eve."

"No, no, no!" everything in my being screamed. "I couldn't possibly sing on Christmas Eve." There was no way I was going to sing. Then I received another letter in the mail. This time it was not from Audrey, but from Brandy. Audrey had done her best to write exactly what Brandy wanted to say.

> *The lights, the tree, the joy, the feeling of the season, for each one of us it is different. Our senses bring back all the memories. Memories of all our past times together will be with you throughout the years.*
>
> *I love you both so much, I can never let you know truly how much love I feel for you. My life with you was beautiful, all the fun we shared together. I took so much for granted. I had so much while many have never felt the joy, not until now. My eyes have opened to the wonder of God, His love can shine through me to you and to others. His love can fill you up with wonder.*

The tree is so beautiful, the candles soft warm glow, the angels dancing through the branches of the tree, all to remind us of the Glory of God. Thank you for making it the most wonderful time for me. Your love reaches me through all of this. I am not gone – I am always there with you. I kiss you on the cheek each day.

I hear your anger and pain, your laughter and joy. I feel all of this. When you have joy and hope in your heart I do also. I am from both of you and from God. I am the tenderness of you Daddy and the joyfulness of you Mother. And I am because of the love of God.

We are all born with a purpose and we each must fulfill that purpose. There are so many children, more than can ever be counted that have never felt the tenderness, joy and love that I have. Our lives are like vines growing – turning each in different directions and following the light to fulfill our purpose. I am still growing and discovering my purpose, and you are finding yours.

Your pain is deep and each day is difficult, but know that each day I am with you. I will always be here until our lives come together again.

I am in the house, in your thoughts, and in your hearts forever – we are always together. You hear my words in the music and for a brief moment you remember how it was. I feel all of this – I am

*there with you. I am within you. I am there with
the angels in the tree, in the light of the candles, and
dancing to the music. I am here at your side. I love
you both so very much and I thank you for the gifts
that you have given me, each one a part of you.*

Merry Christmas Momma and Daddy,
Love Brandy

*P.S. Mother, don't be afraid to sing Silent Night.
I will be there holding your hand. Daddy will you
be there also, we will be together to share our love
for each other.*

That year Christmas Eve was on a Sunday. I went to church
that morning still wondering if I would be able to sing *Silent Night*
at the evening service. It was a cold blustery day and I walked in
the door with my head down trying to protect myself from the
wind and cold. When I finally looked up, I was surprised to see
my friend Tad. Tad had moved from town but we had stayed
in touch, especially after Brandy's death. He had come home to
celebrate Christmas with his family. When he saw me, he said, "I
was hoping you would be here this morning."

Not only is Tad a good friend, he is an excellent singer. I
asked, "Are you going to be here tonight?" He nodded. "Would
you sing with me? I don't know if I can get through the song."
His response was simple, "Absolutely!"

It is amazing when all the pieces just seem to fall into place.
After church we ran through the song a couple of times. On

Christmas Eve we returned to sing one of Brandy's favorite songs about the most important story ever told. Not only did I make it through, I could feel her presence in the sanctuary. On that night I was certain that we were together as a family once again.

Chapter 6

The Woman, the Bush and the Birds

I was not the only one who was struggling to heal and to understand what was going on. Brandy's death had turned Audrey's life upside down as well. Not only was she having experiences that she could not explain, but she was not sure what I needed from her or how to help me find healing. Audrey had not chosen to receive these messages. She marked the first time Brandy appeared to her on the calendar with red pen. She claimed that if she was going insane, she wanted the doctors to have a date when it all started.

Brandy decided it was time for Audrey to start keeping a journal. It was not Audrey's idea. She could never imagine herself as a writer, but Brandy had that way of being persistent when she wanted something. She told her that together they would tell the story. "What story?" Audrey asked her. The story of "The Bush" was the reply, "but that will come later."

Audrey went to the store looking for a little book to begin writing. The only criterion she had was that it have lined paper. She could not write straight without it. It was hard to know where to start, so Brandy told her to start at the beginning. She argued that she could never remember it all, but Brandy promised to help her. I don't know if the journals were more for Audrey or for me. I still keep everything she ever wrote and reread the words often. Not only do they tell a story, but they are filled with wisdom. In one of her early entries she wrote:

> *To begin again is important because I have failed to write the most important words she has ever said to me. On that first day her voice was calm and peaceful. "Love is the most important thing," she said. "With love there is no anger – no hate." At the time I never really understood what she meant. Simple words – no not really. It has taken me awhile to truly understand. Love is the reason we are here on this earth, love is the sun and the rain and this beautiful earth we live on.*

Audrey liked to sit on her back porch and relax. Often it was when her mind was clear and was not consumed with other thoughts that Brandy would speak to her. One spring day Brandy told her it was time to tell the story of "The Bush." The only bush Audrey was aware of was outside her back window. A bird had built a nest and laid some eggs that eventually hatched. Audrey enjoyed listening to the bird family that lived in the bush. Then one day the chirping stopped. Audrey searched the bush but the birds were gone. As Audrey picked up her pencil, it was as if the story was being dictated to her. She thought it was just a simple tale about her backyard. It was not until they were well into the story that Audrey understood it was really about me.

The Woman, the Bush and the Birds

There was an old woman who lived high on a hill above the forest. Her days were filled with work in her garden. She loved being outside in the warm sunshine, watching the birds and forest animals go about their day. The sly fox would watch her work from the ridge above her house. The squirrels and birds chattered about as she trimmed the flowers and cleared the weeds from her garden.

One morning as she opened the window she heard the chirping of little birds. To her surprise she discovered a tiny nest in the small bush outside her window. Her old eyes squinted to focus on the tiny objects inside the nest.

Each day she would carefully open the window to listen to the joyful chirping, being careful not to disturb the busy mother as she went about her work of caring for her young.

The warm sunshine would flow through her window each day as she watched the tiny birds grow. Her heart was filled with joy each time she passed the little bush knowing the precious cargo its branches held.

Early one morning she opened her window, but there was not sound. Suddenly she heard the lone cry coming from the mother bird and she rushed outside to see what was wrong.

The mother bird was flying from tree to tree as if she was wounded and in great pain. The old woman walked to the bush to see if she could help. Maybe the young birds had fallen from the nest. As she pushed the leaves aside to peer into the nest she heard a distinct cry come from the bush.

"'The Thing' has taken the baby birds away!" the bush cried. The old woman could see the nest still there between the branches. The nest was still as it had been before. Nothing had been disturbed. "'The Thing' has taken the baby birds!" the bush cried once again.

"It must be my fault!" the bush wailed. The mother bird continued to thrash about with a piecing cry, flying from tree to tree.

"Why would it be your fault?" the old woman said to the bush, her heart aching at the thought that these tiny creatures were gone.

"I'm too small," the bush replied, "my branches were not strong enough or high enough to keep 'The Thing'" from taking the tiny birds."

The mother landed on a branch near the old woman. "No, no," she said, "it is my fault," her piercing chirps still filling the air. "How could I have been so stupid as to build my nest in such a small tree?"

The old woman looked again searching for an answer. What had taken the tiny birds? They were still too young to fly away. She *searched around, maybe a fox or a snake was nearby, but there was no sign that the nest was disturbed. Where had the tiny birds gone?*

The old woman began to cry, "Why, why, they were so young. They had never learned to fly. They had never left the nest. They had never seen the beauty of the forest and the hills." Her heart was filled with a deep emptiness. How she would miss their little sounds each morning. How could "The Thing" take them away?

The next day the old woman noticed the tiny mother bird sitting on a tree branch not far from the nest. The little mother just sat there not moving as if she was made of stone. As the old woman walked outside she could still hear the swishing cries coming from the little bush. Over and over again, "It is my fault, if only I had been a bigger bush with higher branches."

The old woman walked over to the bush once more checking the nest to see if the tiny creatures had returned, but they were gone—gone. Days, weeks, months passed. Each day she would see the mother bird sitting silently in the tree nearby, and the bush quietly weeping.

As the summer passed and moved into fall, a gentle wind whispered to the bird that her babies were safe in a wonderful place, and that she would see them again. The bird questioned the wind saying, "But what am I to do until this time? I have lost the most precious part of my life."

The wind whispered again that the bird had many purposes, to sail high above in the beautiful sky and to sing each morning, to fill the earth with just being part of creation.

The little bush still filled with sadness and guilt slowly began to die. All the leaves slowly turned brown.

Early the next spring, the old woman noticed the once beautiful bush was all brown and stiff. She slowly trimmed away all the dead leaves and branches, hoping the warm sunshine would renew its spirit. Each day she brought water and would talk to the little bush, pleading with it not to give up.

One day she noticed one tiny branch had started to turn green with a new tiny leaf. It was a sign of hope for the little bush.

I wept when I read the story. The pain was still so near, but I also discovered that the story was true on another level. I had not given up all hope. It was very small, but a tiny green branch was growing in my life.

Chapter 7

Have You Been Baptized?

$\mathscr{I}$ woke up one morning with the name Saint Maria Goretti in my head. It made no sense to me so I called Audrey. I asked her, "What is Saint Maria Goretti? Does that mean anything to you?"

"Yes, she replied, "It is the name of a parish I attended when we lived in Phoenix. It is rather large so we didn't attend long. How do you know about it?"

I didn't know anything about it. In fact I had never heard of it before. There was no reason that name should have been in my head. I asked Audrey if something special was going on in the parish. She did not know, but she would find out. She called her son who still lived in Phoenix and asked him to go over and find out if something was happening at Saint Maria Goretti parish. He was skeptical, but made the journey anyway. When Audrey finally called me back, she simply asked, "How did you know?"

I didn't understand what she meant, so Audrey filled me in. Two girls who had visited Medjugorje were at the parish. I had never heard of Medjugorje, so Audrey explained that it was a little village in Croatia that was similar to Fatima or Lourdes. Again, not being Catholic, these were towns that meant nothing to me. They could have been anywhere in the world. Audrey tried to explain that each of these places was a site where people believed Mary had appeared to children and given them messages. They had become holy sites where many Catholics traveled to hear messages or find healing. The two girls who had returned from Medjugorje were now supposedly hearing messages from Mary. I decided I needed to go to Phoenix. If I was going to believe that Audrey could talk to Brandy, then was it any crazier that these girls were talking to Mary?

I flew to Arizona to meet Audrey, and together we drove a couple of hours to attend a Wednesday evening rosary at Saint Maria Goretti. The parish was huge, and hundreds of people were coming to say the rosary and see the two girls. Outside on the sidewalk, books were being sold that contained messages from the girls. The entire scene reminded me of a carnival. As we milled around, a short little priest wearing a California Highway Patrol cap passed us and said in an Irish accent, "Good evening,

Ladies." I don't remember saying anything, but I am sure Audrey responded with "Good evening, Father."

We headed into the church and found a pew near the back. We still were not sure why we had come, but we knew that we had a two-hour drive to get home that night. We expected to leave the service early and did not want to draw any attention to ourselves when we slipped out.

As the rosary began, I was completely out of my element. There were spoken and sung responses that meant very little to me. It was then that I heard this beautiful tenor voice behind me. When I turned around, it was the little Irish priest we had met outside. He smiled and continued to sing. During the Passing of the Peace, he took my hand and said again, "Good evening."

"You have a nice voice," I responded.

"Thank you, lass," he said holding on to my hand much longer than I expected. I was getting a little uncomfortable as I turned around to sit once again.

As the rosary continued, I was completely lost. I just did not understand it, and when Audrey asked if I was ready to go, I did not hesitate to take the opportunity to slip out quietly. Maybe it had been a mistake to make this trip. What made me believe that I was supposed to travel hundreds of miles to this place?

In the foyer, Audrey took the opportunity to visit the ladies room before our long drive. While I was waiting for her, the same Irish priest approached me again, "Are you leaving, lass?"

"We have to go," I explained. "We have a long drive in front of us."

"Can I interest you in a cup of tea before you go?" he said.

Now he was beginning to make me feel a little more than uncomfortable. What did this priest want from me? I made another attempt to tell him that we needed to go.

"It won't take long," he said calmly. "We can just go over to the rectory."

Finally Audrey returned, and he asked her if we would like to join him for a cup of tea. Audrey declined as well and when he realized that we were serious about leaving, he looked me in the eye and said, "You know your daughter is with the Holy Mother!"

The priest must have seen shock and fear in our eyes, so he calmly invited us one more time to join him for tea. This time we agreed. He took us to the rectory and served us some hot tea. We discovered that his name was Father Paddy and he had come to Phoenix from Ireland as part of some kind of exchange. I was not completely comfortable with the conversation but Father Paddy was very persuasive. He needed to tell me that Brandy was fine and that she was with the Holy Mother. I was still at a time in my life when I cried almost every day and he had one other message for me. "There will be a time when you go to Ireland and you will find peace in your soul."

I don't know if I or Audrey was more shaken by the events of that night. On the ride home she shared with me that she had been Catholic all of her life, but she had never had such an experience. By the time we got back to her house it was late in the evening and we both were exhausted physically and mentally.

Waking the next morning I found Audrey already up. In fact, she was still wearing her clothes from the night before. She had never gone to bed. She had been up all night praying. When she saw me, she said, "Connie, I don't understand so much of this. I had never seen that man before in my life. Before Brandy died, my life seemed so simple. It all made sense. It was as if everything I believed could fit neatly on this little piece of paper. Now I feel like I have one foot here in this world and one foot in another. Am I going crazy?"

Audrey had called her sister before I got up and shared with her the story from the night before. She had expressed the same fears she shared with me, even using the same piece of paper analogy. I asked her how her sister had responded. Audrey said, "She told me I was going to need to get a bigger piece of paper."

During our conversation the phone rang. It was Father Paddy calling to invite me back to Phoenix. To this day I do not know how he found us. Neither of us had given him a telephone number, but I knew one thing, I wasn't ready to talk to him. The situation was very uncomfortable. I gave Audrey the "I'm not here sign," and she told the little priest that I was still in bed. Later we laughed about the whole conversation. If he had the ability to find Audrey's phone number, he could probably figure out that she was lying to him.

Eventually I called Father Paddy out of obligation. I gave him my home phone number and address. During our conversation he asked me "Have you been baptized?" Of course I had been baptized, but he was persistent, "Are you sure?" Father Paddy called and wrote a few more times, and he always asked the same question, "Have you been baptized?"

When I returned home, I went to visit my parents and tell them about my experiences. I don't think they often knew how to respond to my strange stories. They wanted to be supportive, but everything was so far from their reality. I am sure they often wondered if their daughter was going nuts. I decided to ask my mother if I had been baptized. I think she was offended by the question. Of course I had been baptized. All of her daughters were baptized. Why would she have left one of us out? We had attended two different churches, and she could distinctly remember my sister's baptism. She was sure I must have been baptized in a little church we attended on the north side of town.

Just to be sure, I decided to call my childhood church and ask for a copy of my baptism record. I talked to the church secretary whom I had known since childhood. She asked for the date which of course I did not have. She would need to do a little research. When she called back, she had interesting news. She had found a record of my oldest sister's baptism from another church, and my two younger sisters' baptisms from their church, but not mine. They did say that the church had a fire at one time which destroyed some records, but they were quite certain that they had duplicates of everything. They simply had no record that I had ever been baptized.

The next Easter I stood before my church and received baptism. I don't know if the record was lost or if my mother was wrong, but I felt that being baptized was something I was supposed to do. I wrote Father Paddy to let him know that there was no record that I had ever been baptized as a child and that I had received baptism as an adult. Oddly enough, he did not reply and I never heard from him again.

Chapter 8

Medjugorje

$\mathcal{T}$raveling to Phoenix was only the first of my physical journeys searching for spiritual answers that led me to unusual destinations. Each journey has been unexpected and they often seem coordinated by something beyond my comprehension.

One afternoon I was in the grocery store trying to avoid seeing anyone I knew when an old friend came up behind me and asked how I was doing. I still dreaded that question because I was not doing well, but I was tired of talking about it with others. I quickly told her that I was doing okay, and then she made the oddest comment, "I hear you are going to Italy."

Italy! Where in the world did she come up with that idea? I told her, "No, no, you must have me mixed up with someone else."

"I swear I heard it somewhere," she replied.

She could not have heard it somewhere because I had no plans to go to Italy. I hate flying. It is not dying that bothers me, it is crashing. Specifically, knowing that the plane is going to crash and there is nothing I can do about it.

A few days later my friend Gail called. She had been going through a rough time herself and had been invited by her friend Margy to go on a pilgrimage to Medjugorje. She thought I might like to go with her. I had never even heard of Medjugorje until a few months earlier on my trip to Arizona. It seemed like a strange coincidence, but what was really odd is why Gail would want to go. At best you could say she was agnostic. She was the last person I would ever expect to go on a spiritual retreat. Gail was way too cynical.

She probably heard the skepticism in my voice as I questioned why she would go on this trip. Her answer, "I don't know why. All I know is I am supposed to take you!"

There was no way I was going to Croatia. Not only did I hate to fly, but there was a war going on in that part of the world. It made no sense. I politely asked for some details with no intention of ever getting on that plane. Gail did not have many answers, but she would find out from Margy.

When Gail called me back, she had all the information I needed. I was still certain that there was no reason to go until she asked me a question. Gail had never been to Europe before and she had one request. Could we take a few days and go to Italy. This was too much of a coincidence; was somebody trying to tell me something?

I told Mark about the trip and surprisingly he said, "I think you should go." Ever since the night Brandy had appeared to him, he was incredibly supportive of my need to find out more. I asked him if he was worried about the fighting in Bosnia. He said that he would gladly increase my life insurance.

There were still many obstacles before I could leave, including getting a passport in time. I turned it over to God and prayed, "If I am supposed to go, then you are going to have to get me there." I applied for a passport, and miraculously it arrived in four days. Slowly I was running out of excuses.

Gail, Margy and I flew out of Wichita, Kansas, on a chartered plane that was organized by the Medjugorje Mir Center. Gail and I were the only two non-Catholics of the nearly 300 pilgrims on the flight. We had a great time on the plane, but we were constantly asked why we were going if we weren't Catholic. Most of the people had been planning and saving for years just for this moment. They all had stories to tell about why they were going and what they expected. My only answer to their question was, "I don't know."

We landed in Rome in the afternoon and had some time for sight-seeing. We did as many touristy things that we could over the next few hours. Our next plane took off at nine in the evening and flew into Dubrovnik. When we got off the plane, we knew we were not in Kansas anymore. There were soldiers everywhere standing around with machine guns. Going through security took forever as the reality of the war hit us right in the face.

In Dubrovnik we loaded busses to travel the several hours to Medjugorje. It was dark with no street lights for most of the trip. Later I was glad that I could not see the road we traveled or I would have been scared out of my mind. It was as if we were driving on the edge of a cliff. We arrived in Medjugorje at about four in the morning. There are not many hotels in the town and most of us were staying with host families. Gail, Margy and I were assigned to Marjana, one of the six children who saw the apparitions of Mary in 1981 and continued to receive messages for many years. As we got off the bus, Marjana came up and hugged me and said, "You know your child is with the Blessed Mother."

I didn't know how to respond. I had never met this woman in my life and she knew nothing about my family or why I had come to Medjugorje. Gail just looked at me and said, "See, you're supposed to be here."

We spent the next week in Medjugorje walking everywhere. It was absolutely beautiful and very peaceful. Above the town sits Mount Krizevac which means Cross Mountain. In 1933 a 30 ton cross was built on its summit. During harvest time, heavy hailstorms are possible, and the people of the parish wanted some divine protection. All of the cement and sand was carried up the rocky hill by hand, mostly by women and children. Since 1981, the journey to the cross has included the Stations of the Cross.

Margy suggested we do the Stations of the Cross one evening. Not being Catholic, I didn't know what that meant, but I went along with six others. We could see the cross lit up from town, but the journey out was in darkness. We carried flashlights, but I did not realize how far we would be walking. I was not smart enough to wear good hiking shoes and before long I was ready to turn back. We did not seem to be getting any closer, and I was being very vocal about my discomfort. Finally Margy suggested we pray, and she started saying the rosary. In my most sarcastic tone I asked if she was going to rosary up a cab.

Before long, we saw headlights coming up the road. It was almost midnight and I couldn't imagine what car would be out driving, but I was sure it could not hold all seven of us. When the car finally reached us, I was amazed to discover that not only was it a taxi, but it was a Volkswagen bus. The driver asked where we were going and gave us a ride to the foot of Mount Krizevac. We still had two more hours to travel through the Stations of the Cross before we reached the summit, but we had caught our second wind.

As we reached the cross at the top of the mountain, I was surprised to discover that there was no electricity. We had seen the cross from miles away lit up in the night, but the only source of light was the little candles that pilgrims had placed at the foot of the cross. I was sure it had been illuminated by two big spotlights. People were all over bringing their petitions and prayers. I set a picture of Brandy and a prayer petition under one of the candles. By now it was between two or three in the morning. We sat there until the sun came up, and I felt more at peace than I had since before Brandy died. For the first time in what seemed like an eternity, I felt a deep sense of love and contentment with life. I wondered, is this why I am here?

At the end of our stay in Medjugorje, we thanked our hosts and said our goodbyes. I still questioned the purpose of my trip.

Before I boarded the bus, I said to Marjana, "I still don't know why I am here."

She leaned in and replied, "Next time you come, you will know."

Chapter 9

Be Silent Audrey

The first year after Brandy's death I had many experiences that I could not explain. Sometimes I was overwhelmed and I would have to ask myself, "Did that just happen?" All of these experiences were a great mystery, but they were also my lifeline. It was not just Audrey that was giving me messages, but she was my primary source of information. I could never get enough, and I know it created stress for her. We would talk on the phone many times a week, often multiple times in the same day. I would keep her on the phone for hours trying to find out more.

It was not easy for Audrey. She was trying to understand not only what was happening, but also how to share the information with me. I could hear her struggling for the right words, trying not to misinterpret the message. I was often impatient with her, even taking my anger out on her. I wanted her to talk to Brandy whenever I asked. Audrey tried to explain that it did not work that way. She had to wait for Brandy and the messages were not always clear.

After the first year, Audrey and I went through periods of silence. I would call and Audrey would have nothing to tell me. Eventually she stopped answering her phone as if she were avoiding me. I would leave messages, but days would pass before she returned my call. I don't blame her; I was so needy and she knew I would be disappointed if there was no word from Brandy. What I did not understand was that the silence was intentional. I already knew everything I needed to understand to begin my healing. Brandy was okay and I would see her again. What I needed was to start living my life again. Audrey finally sent me a letter explaining what was going on.

Connie and Mark,

I am very sorry if my silence has hurt you. I told her that you would be angry with me and her words were the same, "Be silent Audrey." She told me that I would know when the time was right and this morning the words started flowing again. I thought it would be easier to call but she said to write it down. She said that I was a cord that tied you to her and that my silence was important. She says for you both to search in your hearts to find the strength to carry on your lives. I wish I could find the words that would give you the feeling of how much she loves you both, but I will never be able to capture it. It soars like an eagle in flight over the highest mountain and shines like the brightest sun. Her sorrow for you is very deep. This is the first time she has really cried. She has said that it is okay for us to disagree with one another but we must treat each other with dignity and respect in spite of our anger. She does not want me to tie the cord between us too tight or close because she continues to say that you must make the decisions for your life. This has been hard for me whether you believe it or not. I have said before that I do not like being in other people's lives. I will continue to write when she talks to me. I realize that all of this at times seems so unreal, it does for me anyway. I know that this past year for me has been the most joyful and full of peace. I wish I could share it with you. My belief and love in God has become stronger and Brandy has helped me achieve this. But she is with God and all goodness comes from Him. Even though I do not always understand, my faith continues. I pray that you both find this peace and joy in your life. She told me always to search in my heart for the right answer. Her words are always with me. You have a very special daughter.

Included in her letter was a message from Brandy for both Mark and I. It began with an introduction from Audrey.

Dearest Connie and Mark,

I would like both of you to read this. Please know that if you have ever believed what I have told you in the past, listen to her words now.

My heart has ached for both of you. I see the turmoil in your lives, the anger, but you must be responsible for you own lives. I watch as you hurt one another but in it all there is a need for you both because of me. I am part of both of you, created by God and now I am of Him.

Mother, we were so close – two vines yet both growing so close together it was difficult to see that we were separate. My life was yours and yours mine. You are strong and you must carry on without me. I will be at your side always, but you must live your life now without me. I cannot make decisions for you or lead your life, but I will always be with you.

Daddy, I love you very much. You are so kind and gentle. You too must find the strength within yourself and know that I am always with you – always. I want your lives to be full and happy and loving and when it is time we will be together again.

The most important thing now is our love for one another. This bond will never disappear. It is like a star always shining in the dark of night.

Love,
Brandy

Some of the things that Audrey had to say to me were hard to hear. How could she have so much joy and peace when I was still experiencing so much pain? I did not want her to stay silent, even if it was for my own good. Still, as much as I hated to admit it, she was right. It was time for me to start living my life again. I was depending too much on Audrey. She had her life to live and I had mine. What I feared the most was not the separation from Audrey, but losing my connection to Brandy through Audrey. I didn't want her to be silent. I never considered Brandy might find others paths to communicate with me.

Chapter 10

Unexpected Visitor

A new path opened when I received a call one afternoon from the Director of the Medjugorje Mir Center in Wichita. We had met a few years earlier when I traveled on my pilgrimage to Medjugorje. She needed a favor. One of the child visionaries from the village, Ivan, had grown up and married a girl from Boston. They lived in Europe, but periodically they would visit the United States. On these trips Ivan would travel around the country visiting Catholic churches and cathedrals. He did not drive himself but depended on churches to provide travel and lodging.

I was overjoyed at the opportunity; I just could not understand why I was chosen to pick him up an hour and a half away, bring him back to my home, provide him a place to stay, feed him and transport him to the Catholic Cathedral in town. I don't know how many Catholics live in town, but we have three Catholic churches. I am sure that there were hundreds of people that would have jumped at the chance to provide hospitality for Ivan.

At the time, Ivan was still receiving daily messages from the Blessed Mother. Wherever he was at 6:00 p.m., he would stop what he was doing, start the rosary and Mary would appear to him. My job was simply to bring him to town, get him dinner and make sure he was at the Cathedral before six o'clock. The Director of the Mir Center would meet us there.

When I met Ivan, I was surprised at how normal he seemed. I don't know what I expected but I was surprised that there was nothing extraordinary about him. He was not arrogant or self-centered and obviously lived a simple, humble life. He also had a terrible cold so even though he spoke some English, we did not spend a lot of time talking on the trip home. I think he just wanted to rest.

I took Ivan to cathedral early so he could be in the sanctuary at six o'clock. The church was filled with people, many of whom came from out of town hoping to have an experience of something holy. Ivan was sitting up front when the congregation started saying the rosary. Suddenly his expression changed. I didn't see anything, but there was a feeling in the air. I knew something was happening. At that moment Ivan looked as if he were completely oblivious that anyone else was in the cathedral. He was obviously talking to someone although it was not a conversation that was audible to anyone around him.

I found myself more interested in watching the people in the sanctuary than Ivan. In the last few years I had witnessed many things I never anticipated, but I was still well out of my comfort zone. This was so far from the way I was raised as a good little protestant girl. Many of my non-Catholic friends that were sitting nearby were having similar experiences. Something was happening, but there was no tangible proof. I wanted desperately to see something, to have an experience that I could point to and say, "See, I am not out of my mind, these things happen to other people too!" And then it was over, there wasn't anything else. Ivan sat back down and we dismissed to the fellowship area for a meet and greet.

After the events of the evening I invited many of my friends to come back to my house for an informal reception. Ivan was still quite ill and did not feel like being very social. He retreated to the family room, sat down on the couch and turned on a basketball game. He didn't seem to have any need to impress the people that had come to see him. Again I was surprised at how normal this man appeared. He was just a simple, humble man who was living a fascinating life.

People really wanted to talk to Ivan, but I did not want to impose upon him while he was feeling so poorly. I did walk into the room to offer him a drink or see if he needed anything. He stopped watching the television for a moment, looked me right in the eye, grabbed my arm and said in his Bosnian accent, "Tomorrow night when I talk to the Blessed Mother, I will inquire about your daughter."

I was completely caught off guard by his unexpected response. I had not approached him to ask about Brandy. It was the first time he had spoken to me so directly and with such purpose. I probably said something like thank you or that would be nice, but I honestly don't remember saying anything. Finally he said, "I will have some hot tea." Then he turned back around and continued watching his game.

Eventually my guests left for the evening and we retired for the night. Ironically, Ivan stayed in Brandy's room. The next morning someone else came to pick him up and drive him to his next destination, another town in Kansas where he would be involved in a similar worship experience.

The entire next day, I tried to find things to distract my mind, but it was hard not to think about what Ivan had said the previous night. I made sure that I was home near the phone by six o'clock. There was no way I was going to miss that call. It was about 9:45 that evening when I finally received a call from the Director of the Mir Center with a message from Ivan. His message from Mary was: *My Dear Child – Your Mother will pray for you in a special way and will intercede to my son. Brandy is together with me. She is safe. Brandy is saying to her mother, "Mama, don't be afraid of anything. I'm praying for you and dad."* It wasn't earth-shattering or even something tangible that I could show to someone else, but it was enough. Once again I found peace that my daughter was okay and the assurance that she would find new avenues to make her presence known.

Chapter 11

Another Christmas

$\mathcal{M}$ark and I have carried on with our lives as Brandy requested, but the holidays never get any easier, no matter how much time goes by. Christmas is especially hard to endure because everyone else seems to be enjoying the holiday and all I can do is think about what is missing. Three and a half years after Brandy's death I was deep in my Christmas funk. Mark was working hard at the restaurant and one night had some catering to deliver. I am not a bubble bath person, but for some reason I decided that is exactly what I needed.

I had some new lavender soap that I wanted to try so I filled the tub, lit some candles, turned on the Christmas music and settled in for my own personal pity party. All I really wanted to do was rewind time. As I started to use my new soap, I felt something hard on my upper chest. I compared it to the other side which just felt like normal flesh. I don't know why, but it didn't register that something might be wrong; it was just odd.

A few weeks later I had a doctor's appointment which included a mammogram. The x-ray technician asked if I had any concerns and I told her that I did not. She did seem to be taking more pictures than usual, but her explanation was that since we were so close to Christmas she wanted to get every angle possible. Everybody was going on vacation soon so it would be difficult to return to take more pictures if necessary.

She asked again if I had any concerns so I told her about the hard spot on my chest. I said, "It doesn't hurt, but feel this." After examining the area, she decided that even more pictures were needed. Now rather nervous, I asked if she saw anything. I don't know if she would have told me at that time, but her answer was that she just wanted to be sure. I scheduled a follow-up appointment the next day.

When I walked into my doctor's office the next morning, I nonchalantly asked how he was doing. His quick answer was "I'm fine but you're not!" There was no easing into the bad news or a gentle "I have some concerns." He was very direct as if every second counted. He put my films up on the wall and pointed out a large tumor in my upper left breast. He explained that it was very aggressive and needed to come out immediately. There was no doubt in his mind that it was malignant. He had already set up an appointment later in the day with a surgeon and told me that I needed to bring Mark with me.

The surgeon was a family friend whom I trusted completely. When Mark and I showed up in his office that afternoon, I could tell he was worried. He showed me more pictures of the tumor and agreed with the original diagnosis. The tumor was large and aggressive. It was already growing fingers that were reaching out to infect other parts of my body. There was no time to make decisions. He had scheduled surgery for 7:00 a.m. the next morning. I argued that the next day was Christmas Eve; couldn't we wait until after the holiday. Surely he didn't want to work the day before Christmas. He was adamant; the tumor needed to be removed immediately. I knew if he was willing to work on Christmas Eve, then my condition must be serious.

Since Brandy's death I spent most days not caring if I lived or if I died. Now with the diagnosis of aggressive breast cancer I could hear God saying, "Here is your out. If you want to die, all you have to do is nothing. The cancer will do it for you."

I looked at my doctor and asked if the treatment was just surgery or if it would include chemotherapy. You have to understand that I don't do puke. I have a great aversion to vomit, whether it is my own or someone else's. In our family it has always been Mark's job to deal with puke. Chemo could be the deal breaker on the entire treatment plan. All the doctor had to do was say the word "puke" and I was done.

My doctor explained that with an aggressive tumor like the one they had found, not only would I need surgery and chemotherapy, but the treatment would also include radiation. That was all I needed to hear. This was my chance to throw in the towel, but I shocked myself with my response. Out of my mouth came the word "Okay."

I had one more question; would the surgery take the whole breast or just the lump? I was given the option to remove only the tumor, but I needed more information. I asked my doctor if it were his wife what he would do. He said that he would take the whole breast, so I said, "Take them both. There is no reason to walk around lop-sided." He thought maybe I should slow down and think about that, but there was nothing to think about; as far I was concerned, he just needed to do it.

The hardest part was not going through with the surgery, it was telling my parents. They were so fragile from their other losses. Mark and I decided we needed to talk to them together. We sat down around the dining room table and I shared our bad news. Mom started to cry and Daddy added one more reason to be angry with God. It is almost as hard to watch your parents hurt as it is to watch your children hurt. It is such a helpless feeling.

I know many women who go home after they have received the news about cancer and research everything they can about the disease. Not only do they want to be well informed about the things they will face, but they look up doctors and their records before making a decision about their treatment. I didn't do any of that. I went home and set the table for Christmas dinner. I got the coffee pots ready to plug in, rolled the silverware with ribbons and made sure everything was in place. It was all pretty brainless, but I didn't sit around and worry about the cancer.

The day of my surgery, the pre-op room was filled with family and friends. Only emergency surgeries are scheduled on Christmas

Eve, so we had the run of the hospital. As the people closest to me gathered around, many of them were crying but I was remarkably calm. I had this strange peace that I was going to be okay. I felt as if I were in a bad movie where I already knew the outcome. My fear was not death; it was getting sick from the treatment. That morning I was much more worried about my parents and their pain than anything I was about to face.

Don't get me wrong; cancer treatment is no day at the park. I have heard many patients say that if they had truly understood everything that they were about to experience, they might have chosen another option. The lump was removed from my breast on Christmas Eve, and two weeks later I had a second surgery to remove both breasts. For the next ten months I endured chemotherapy and radiation treatments to kill any remaining cancer cells.

The cancer and the treatment took a tremendous toll on my body, but I discovered something amazing through the process. I had decided to fight the cancer. This was a remarkable turn of events. I was not as anxious to die as I had thought I was. For the first time since Brandy's death, I wanted to live. Not only had the cancer been removed from my body, but the cancer in my spirit was beginning to heal as well. It was important that my body and spirit would regain strength because Mark and I were about to face another challenge in our lives.

Chapter 12

You Figure it Out!

The Brookville Hotel has been in Mark's family for four generations. As far as I can tell, the Kansas Pacific Railroad built it as a hotel in 1870. It was designed as a bunkhouse for the railroad workers. In 1895, Mark's great-grandparents bought the hotel, and twenty years later his grandmother started serving homemade fried chicken on weekends. Word began to spread and eventually the food became more popular than the rooms. The hotel continued operation until 1972 when it stopped renting rooms, but the restaurant has been serving fried chicken meals for nearly 100 years. It was Brandy's desire to take over the family business some day.

The restaurant was located in a small Kansas town and the sewage system had been an ongoing issue. Over the years

I estimate that we spent nearly $100,000 trying to solve the problem, but there was not a good solution. There was no city sewer and the restaurant was landlocked. We could not build a retention pond nearby. Every possibility we looked at was filled with complications. Finally we realized we were out of affordable options.

The Brookville Hotel in Abilene

In 1999 the state of Kansas inspected the situation and concluded that not only was the sewage system inadequate, but it was also illegal. They gave us a time frame to work with the town to fix the problem. The town did not want to spend the money to build an adequate sewage system and we could not afford it. We were faced with the real possibility that after over 85 years of serving homemade fried chicken dinners, the Brookville Hotel would be closing its doors.

After everything we had been through in the previous four years, I wondered how much more I could take. Why was God punishing me? I was still grieving the death of my sister and my only daughter. My recovery from breast cancer was not complete and now the only stability in my life, our family business, was about to be taken away. What had I done to deserve this? What had Brandy done to deserve this? I was mad at everyone, especially God. I finally cried out to God and said, "I'm done! You figure it out and then let me know!"

Within a few days a series of events began to take place that I could have never imagined. A local radio personality from a nearby town began talking about our restaurant. He had heard of our dilemma and the decision to close our doors. He decided that people needed to know what was about to happen so he took it upon himself to get the word out through the radio waves. Before long we began receiving phone calls from other communities all asking the same question. "Would we be willing to relocate to a new town?"

We must have visited five or six different cities that were making serious bids to bring our restaurant to town. There were many factors to consider including cost of relocation, visibility and distance from our current home. I was overwhelmed by the possibilities and once again I called out to God, "You figure it out and let me know!"

Mark and I had been having many conversations about the future of the Brookville Hotel when we received a call from Abilene, a medium-sized Kansas town just off Interstate 70. I was still in the middle of my cancer treatments, but we decided to drive to Abilene and take a look. Most of the town sat south of the interstate, but there were plans to develop streets to the north where city officials were suggesting we build. There were no structures yet, and as we drove around we found a small cemetery. Suddenly Mark hit the brakes. On the property next to the cemetery was a small grotto with a statue of Mary and a young girl kneeling. I immediately cried out, "That's Bernadette!"

The Grotto we found in Abilene

Bernadette is the young girl who had visions of the Virgin Mary at Lourdes in the 1800's. One day I was in a music store hoping to find some music to connect with Brandy. Audrey was always telling me songs that Brandy wanted me to hear. I wondered if Brandy could do the same for me. I stood in the store trying to listen for her voice that would direct me to a new song, but I was getting nothing. Finally I picked up a CD by Aaron Neville and bought it because it had a version of the Lord's Prayer. When I got home, it was another song that captured my heart. Called *Song of Bernadette*, it told the story of a young girl.

There was a child named Bernadette
I heard the story long ago
She saw the queen of heaven once
And kept the vision in her soul
No one believed what she had seen
No one believed what she heard
That there were sorrows to be healed
And mercy, mercy in this world

So many hearts I find
Broke like yours and mine
Torn by what we've done and can't undo
I just want to hold you
Come on, let me hold you
Like Bernadette would do

We've been around, we fall, we fly
We mostly fall, we mostly run
And every now and then we try
To mend the damage that we've done
Tonight, tonight I just can't rest
I've got this joy right here inside my breast
To think that I did not forget
That child, that song of Bernadette

So many hearts I find
Broke like yours and mine
Torn by what we've done and can't undo
I just want to hold you
Come on, let me hold you
Like Bernadette would do[5]

I don't know why I knew the statue was Bernadette, but I did. Mark turned to me and said, "This is where we are supposed to be."

We set up a meeting with a group of city leaders and asked about the property. At one time a Catholic orphanage had existed in the area, but it closed in 1952. The location where we would build had been used as a dairy farm to support the orphanage. Audrey had told me many times that Brandy is working with the Virgin Mary to take care of the children, especially children that have not been so lucky to be loved. We knew that this was the right place, but would the land even be for sale and would we be able to afford it?

**The former Catholic Orphanage closed in 1952
and has since been torn down**

The property owner was contacted and we planned a dinner at our restaurant for him along with the mayor and members of the city's economic development team. It was an opportunity to share our story and our desire to move to a new location. We wanted him to see that we were serious, and we needed to put a human face on our business.

A few days later we received a call from our attorney. He had a letter we needed to read from the owner of the property. An offer had been made to sell us the land for ten dollars. My first question was, "What does he want?"

Our lawyer replied, "I don't think he wants anything. I have read this letter ten times and the only thing he requests is the property back if you decide not to build. He has given you 18 months to secure financing. Connie, I don't get it. This simply does not happen."

I could not believe that there was not a catch so I called the gentleman myself and invited him to dinner. I asked him to explain to me why he would sell us valuable property for literally nothing. He said to me, "I don't know for sure, but your story touched my life. I didn't know your daughter, but as I drove home from your restaurant the other night I asked myself what I would do if I lost a child. I have three children and I can't imagine losing any of them. When I arrived home, I got down on my hands and knees and I asked God what I could do to help these people pick up the broken pieces of their lives. You may not believe this but when I was done, I sat down and typed you a letter. I didn't even know what it said so I showed it to my wife. Her only response, 'When the Lord speaks, you don't ask questions.' It wasn't me, Connie. I have never done anything like this before."

Within days we secured financing and signed the papers. What only a few weeks earlier had seemed impossible was now becoming a reality. We were about to start a whole new chapter in our lives. Then one day we received a phone call from the man who sold us the property. "Connie, I have good news and bad news. If I could write my dream job… well, it has just been offered to me in California. What is worse is that they are paying me a sinful amount of money to take it. I am moving to the West Coast." This man had come into our lives, given us an unimaginable gift and then moved on just as quickly. I don't know how prayer normally works, but sometimes when you are at the end of your rope and have no place left to turn, God has things that you never imagined just around the corner.

Chapter 13

The Red Bird

Moving the restaurant was much harder than I expected. It didn't help that we were borrowing more money than I could ever imagine in order to re-create the same building in a new location, but I had finally come to peace that we were doing the right thing. The hard part was all the memories at our old place. Brandy had spent many hours growing up at the restaurant; it was her home. She had never been to the new building, so I wondered if I would be losing part of her in this move. Audrey called to tell me what I already knew; I didn't need to worry about Brandy. She would be going with us to our new location. Then she said that if I needed to be reminded, I should plant a tree for her and make it an evergreen.

I put a lot of thought into what kind of tree I wanted to plant. I finally settled on a blue spruce. I thought it would be a beautiful, majestic tree, but when it arrived it was far from majestic. It was spindly and pathetic, not symmetrical at all. Mark said he thought it looked like a dancer which was appropriate for Brandy. Within six months, however, it had lost all of its color. I called the county extension office to check the soil. They gave us some suggestions and for awhile the tree got taller, but it was still pathetic.

Soon after we planted the tree, I was at work when I heard someone come in the front door. It was the owner of a local gift store where I liked to shop for handmade jewelry. Nervously she handed me a package saying, "I was asked to give you this."

I was a little surprised. I wondered for a moment if I had bought something in her store and forgot. Maybe someone was sending me a gift, but I thought it was odd for the owner to make a special trip to give it to me. I asked her if I was supposed to open the package. She nodded. Inside the box, I found a little green and white silver bracelet. Hanging from the bracelet was a small evergreen charm.

I looked at her and said, "Who is this from? Did someone buy it for me?"

"No," she replied.

I kept looking at her, waiting for a better answer. This made absolutely no sense. Finally I asked, "Do you know my daughter?"

Quietly she responded, "We've met."

I must have had an incredible look of disbelief on my face and blurted out, "We planted an evergreen in the yard for her."

"I know," she stopped me. "She loves you very much." She turned around and quietly left the restaurant to return to her shop.

The Evergreen charm

A few years later we had a new visitor at the restaurant. We have two large windows that face the parking lot, and one afternoon before the dinner rush we heard a loud thud against one of the windows. I went to investigate and found a mark on the window. Below it, lying on the grass, was a red bird, so still that it appeared severely injured or even dead. A little later we heard another thud and when I checked, the bird was again lying in the grass. By the time we could go outside, the bird was no longer in the grass but sitting on top of Brandy's tree. One of my employees looked at me and said, "Maybe it is Brandy."

I looked at her disgusted, replying, "My daughter is not a bird."

The red bird hung around for days. It would sit in the window by the cash register and look at us. I had never seen a bird do that before, but it seemed very interested in activities going on in the restaurant. Mark was very frustrated with the bird as it left droppings everywhere. He was sure that she had built a nest in the eves, but he could never find one.

The red bird was a constant at the restaurant. One afternoon I was having lunch with a friend in the dining room when the bird flew up to the window. My friend started talking to the bird and then turned to me and said, "She just came by to say 'Hello, Mom.'" Another time I walked out to the parking lot when the red bird flew to my car and perched on the side view mirror. It leaned way over as if it were looking in the mirror just as Brandy used to do.

Others kept making the connection between the red bird and Brandy, but I was not. Brandy was not a bird. I finally told someone that if the bird shows up at my house, I might believe. A week later we were having a cookout to celebrate my birthday. I called Mark to tell him that I would pick him up at the house. As I pulled in the driveway, I looked up to see a red bird sitting on our yard lamp as if to say "Happy Birthday, Mom!"

For my birthday, Mark gave me a gift certificate to the gift shop where I had received my evergreen bracelet. I did not need any more jewelry, but I did want a nice flower arrangement to put in one of our bathrooms. I went to see the owner and gave her some ideas for what I wanted. She said she would work on it and give me a call when it was done. A few days later it was ready and I stopped by to take a look. It was exactly what I wanted, a flower arrangement that was the right size and color for my house. Then after a closer inspection I saw hanging amidst the flowers, a little red bird. When I looked at the shop owner, she just smiled. I asked, "Have you had company?"

She took me to a back room where she could tell me the story. She explained, "Last night I was working late. It was close to midnight and I was tired when Brandy started in. She asked me to do her a favor and put a red bird in the flowers for her mother. I told her that I didn't have a red bird in the store, but she insisted that I did. I would find it in the Christmas clearance stuff. I argued with her, but she was very adamant that it was there. She was right. She then asked me to give you this message, 'Everything in its right time.'"

I asked her what that meant. She said, "I don't know, but I think it means you should stop worrying so much."

Chapter 14

Mystery Friend

Not everyone was ready to believe the stories that were happening in my life. I could understand why some were skeptical. Belief in an after-life is always a step of faith. We want to believe that there is life after death. Our religion teaches us that life does not end, but if we are honest we have to admit that we won't truly know until our lives come to an end. We are afraid to believe something that we cannot prove. Even with all of my experiences I still questioned what I believed. Were these things really happening or was I just imagining them because I needed them to happen?

I am not very good at keeping my mouth shut, so I was unafraid to share my story. Some of my friends were very supportive and at least pretended to believe I was telling the truth. Others tried to be nice, but I could tell that they thought I was perhaps a little nuts. No one ever said it to me directly but they didn't have to. I could read it in their body language and in their hesitant responses. My parents were somewhere in the middle. I know they were hurting as badly as I was by the losses they had endured. They wanted to believe that Brandy and my sister were okay and in the promise of eternal life, but they were just such practical people. They were not going to jump head first into the great mysteries of life.

In one of my conversations with Audrey, she mentioned that someone else was appearing with Brandy. She didn't have many details, but she believed that they had become friends. She wondered if I knew anyone in Brandy's life named Robert who had died recently. I tried desperately to come up with someone but without any luck. Of course, I wanted more details. What did he look like? How did she know him? Why was he hanging around my daughter? Audrey didn't have many details to give. All she knew is that his name was Robert, and he had sandy-colored hair with big curls. The curls were so big that it reminded her of a time when men wore wigs.

The details about Robert came very slowly. Eventually Audrey added a second name, Steven. Over a period of months she got more information which she would relay to me. It was like a puzzle we were trying to solve. One day she called and gave me the name Wakefield. There is a Kansas town by that name, so I asked her if that is what she meant. Audrey didn't know for sure, but she didn't think it had anything to do with the town. Other clues kept coming in. *Anne of Green Gables* was mentioned, a book that Brandy loved as a child. Audrey also thought there was a connection to Nova Scotia and Boston or Massachusetts.

More and more curious, I wanted to know who this mystery man was that had entered my daughter's life. I continued to ask Audrey what he looked like. One afternoon she was walking through the mall and saw a movie poster for *George of the Jungle*. She called me and said, "Robert looks like Brendon Frasier, the guy who plays *George of the Jungle*, only with sandy-colored, curly hair."

Thinking the library might hold some answers, I scoured atlases to find towns named Wakefield, and found many in the United States. I also found one in Canada which seemed to be a potential connection because of some of the other clues. When I called the city for more information, I discovered that the people spoke only French. Perhaps this path was leading nowhere.

A call from Audrey set matters straight. As she was driving home one day, she almost wrecked her car. Robert had appeared like a movie in her windshield, saying clearly, "My name is Wakefield." It would have been nice if he could have told her that earlier, but for some reason he decided to wait until he could put her life in danger to share that information. I asked if she had received any more clues. She believed he had some connection to furniture, possibly wicker furniture. Then she added the name Cyrus. She didn't know why the name Cyrus, but she was hearing it loud and clear.

I did not have a computer in those days and had no idea how to use one, but one of Brandy's friends offered to help me do some research on her computer. She began putting some of the words I had into a search engine, trying different combinations of words like Nova Scotia, Robert Steven Wakefield, Boston, Massachusetts, wicker furniture and Cyrus. A web site on the history of wicker furniture contained this paragraph:

> *While the first items of wicker furniture came to America with travelers on the Mayflower, it would not experience widespread popularity in the new world until the mid-nineteenth century. Rattan, the most common material for wicker furniture, was frequently used in this time period to hold cargo in place on trading ships that had ventured to Asia. In the early 1850s, Cyrus Wakefield, now considered the father of American wicker furniture, discovered large quantities of rattan on the shipping docks of Boston and became fascinated by the material (Saunders 1990). Recognizing rattan's potential for a variety of purposes, Wakefield began his own rattan importing company in Boston and commenced bringing entire ships full of it into America. The material became quite popular with basket and furniture makers, and Wakefield himself began constructing his own line of wicker furniture from rattan. His popular furniture designs soon caught on and his company became the industry leader in wicker furniture.*

I screamed when I read it. The pieces were beginning to fall into place. As we researched further, we discovered that his factory was in a town ten miles north of Boston called Wakefield. Originally it was known as South Reading. The town voted to change its name in 1868 when Cyrus Wakefield offered to build a new town hall.

I printed off all the material we had found and took it to my parents. I can still remember where they were when I drove up to the house. Mom was sitting on the porch swing and Daddy was raking the yard. I told them the story of the mystery man that Audrey had seen with Brandy and all the clues they had given us. Then I showed them the information we had found. For the first time I could tell that they were starting to believe the stories I had been telling them. It was getting harder to deny that my experiences might be real.

Just finding information about Cyrus Wakefield on the computer was not enough for me. I needed to see for myself. I invited Brandy's friend to go with me as she was now a part of this puzzle. The biggest challenge was finding a time we could both go because she was a college student and I had a restaurant to run. Our window of opportunity was in August so I made reservations at a hotel. Then Audrey called. "Brandy says you should wait six months." Six months! I couldn't wait six months. Besides it would be the middle of winter, an awful time to visit Massachusetts. We ignored her and went anyway.

Wakefield is a cute little town, a suburb of Boston with a population around 25,000. We flew into Boston and took a cab to our Wakefield hotel. I was anxious to find the town library so we could do more research. Audrey had shared with me that Robert was a relative of Cyrus. This information bothered me a little. I was still being a protective mom. How old was this man who was now hanging out with my daughter?

At the hotel I asked how far we were from downtown. It was within walking distance and the day was beautiful. We enjoyed our walk through picturesque town, finally reaching the library. It was surrounded by scaffolding and on the door a sign disclosed, "Closed for Renovation – Open in January." We just started laughing. Obviously, we should have waited six months. Returning to the hotel by cab, we noticed a sign on the building across the street: "Temporary Library." We could have saved a lot of time if we had read the sign earlier. At least we got some good exercise and some fresh air.

The following morning we ventured across the street and entered the library to find some books on the history of Wakefield, Cyrus or his furniture factory. The very pleasant librarian inquired if we were descendants of the Wakefield family. We told her we were not, and she led us to some books on the factory, the town square and the family home. The library was not busy, so the librarian returned after a time to see if we had found everything. We asked, "Is the furniture factory or the Wakefield mansion still around?"

"I'm sorry," she shared, "the mansion burned down and not much is left of the factory."

"Is there an address where they once stood?" we asked.

"Of course," she said, "but how will you get there? Do you have a car?"

"We can take a cab," I replied.

"You don't need to do that," she said. "I will take you."

Our new friend took us all over Wakefield showing us the historical sites and filling us in on the history of the furniture factory. Many of the workers came from Nova Scotia, traveling by boat to the Boston area to find jobs. The Wakefield Furniture Company had been the main employer in town. Several times our hostess asked why we were so interested in her town and the history. I sensed Brandy's friend thinking to herself, "Oh no, she is going to tell her!" At lunch together when she asked a third time why we were so interested in her community, I told her my story. It didn't phase her one bit. I asked her if she had any genealogical records of the Wakefield family. She did, but they were in the basement of the library. She would not have access to them for – six months!

That night I called Audrey to tell her about our day. She had more information for us that was now making sense. For some time she had been given the name Mary Harnecke. She thought that Mary was Robert's mother, although the last names were different. Mary was from Nova Scotia and she came to work as a servant in the Wakefield home. After she became pregnant by one of the men in the home, they sent her back to Nova Scotia. Robert was her illegitimate child. Audrey did not believe that Cyrus was his father, but he was related. Robert eventually returned to Wakefield where he worked in the family business.

I don't know how two spirits born over 100 years apart came together on the other side, but I know that I could not have made any of this up. Even my most skeptical friends were starting to believe that I might not be completely mad. Taking that trip and finding the clues to solve the mystery was a journey of validation. It allowed me to open myself to new possibilities in my own life.

Chapter 15

Becoming a Messenger

I have often wondered how Audrey found the courage to make the first phone call to me sharing that she had a message from Brandy. I have to believe that if Brandy had not been so persistent, Audrey would have never picked up the phone. It is like the little boy in the movie *The Sixth Sense* who tells Bruce Willis, "I see dead people." Seeing dead people makes for great entertainment, but in the real world it just makes people think you are weird.

As far as I know, Audrey had never had such experiences before Brandy's death. I believe she always had the ability, but she was just not consciously aware of it. Once Brandy was able to make the connection, other spirits began talking to Audrey. I think she wondered if those who have passed on have their own little grapevine to spread the news that a new line has opened up to our world.

Audrey called me one afternoon to ask if I knew a specific family in town. Their son had recently been killed in a car accident. She had known the young man as a child. He had lived nearby and was involved in a neighborhood carpool. Audrey described his parents as acquaintances but not close friends. She had not seen the family in years and would have never felt comfortable calling them on the phone.

When Audrey called that day, she asked if I had heard about the car accident. It had been in the news so I was aware of the story, but I had never met the family. I would have barely recognized them if I saw them in a store. Audrey wondered if the boy's mother liked to sew because her son kept coming to her, especially when she would sit down at the sewing machine. I asked if Brandy was with him, but she said that she wasn't. I asked if they knew each other and she said that she didn't know. Why she was telling me all of this?

The young man had an important request for Audrey: "Can you let my mother know that I am okay? She is not doing well." My mind flashed back to years earlier when Brandy had died. Even though the pain never goes away, I had found some healing over time. In the first weeks and months the pain was so intense that I did not want to live. If there was anyone who could understand what this woman was going through, it was me. During that time, Audrey had been my life-line. As hard as it was for her to make that call to me, it was worth the risk. Now she needed to connect with this boy's mother. If there was a chance she could bring some comfort and healing to her life, then she needed to try.

Audrey understood the need to talk to the boy's mother, but she was hesitant to do it herself. Instead she had something else in mind. "Connie, I can't do it. I have not seen this woman in years. I cannot call her." It was hard enough for her to call a friend and risk letting her think she was crazy. There was no way she was going to be that vulnerable with someone who was nearly a complete stranger.

The young man was persistent, maybe not as persuasive as Brandy, but he continued to appear to her. He did not always ask her if she would talk to his mother, but Audrey was often aware of his presence. She continued to tell him that she could not do what he was asking. Finally he made a new request, "Will Mrs. Martin talk to my mother?"

For the first time I was beginning to understand what it was like to be Audrey. How was I supposed to tell a complete stranger that I had a message from her dead son? Where do you start a conversation like that? Believing that Brandy was talking to my friend was one thing. Taking the risk of talking to a grieving mother was something completely different. I was not comfortable becoming the messenger, but something was compelling me. I remembered how hearing that my daughter was okay had made a difference in my life. I realized that I had a responsibility to try.

I called the mother of this young man and made an appointment to come see her. She was a counselor, and I am sure she thought I was calling to talk about some issue in my life. She agreed to see me at her house. As I sat in her living room, I remember wondering where I should start. I finally said, "We have a mutual friend." I told her about Audrey and how they had been in a neighborhood carpool for their children. She remembered Audrey living on the same street. So far so good, but it was time to take a leap of faith.

I took a deep breath and started telling my story about Brandy. I cannot remember all the details of that day; I was so nervous that most of it was a blur. I do know that at one point I shared that I had a message from her son that had come through Audrey. I was smart enough to write it all down because I would have never kept it straight, so I just started to read. At one point I told her that she had seen her son recently near the park. She began to sob, nodding as she said, "I saw him in his car and he was wearing . . . " I finished her sentence for her, ". . . a white shirt and sunglasses."

It was in that moment that I could see something was confirmed in this grieving mother. The day she was remembering had been particularly difficult. She had called in sick at work because she could not bear facing anyone. While driving near a park, she looked up and thought she saw her son driving his car and wearing a white shirt and sunglasses. Later that day her daughter called with her own story. At almost exactly the same time in a city hundreds of miles away, she thought she saw her brother driving his car and wearing a white t-shirt and sunglasses.

I shared everything else in the message I had written down from Audrey. Mostly I wanted this woman to hear that her son was well and that he loved her very much. She offered me a glass of Pepsi and we sat there, talking and crying with one another. All of a sudden her husband pulled into the driveway and a look of panic came across her face. She literally ripped the cup I was drinking out of my hand and said, "He can't find me like this, he will not tolerate the tears." She opened the door and said goodbye. It was an abrupt ending to a stressful yet satisfying afternoon.

I never heard from the woman again. I didn't expect to, I wasn't planning on becoming good friends. My job was simply to be a messenger of hope. As hard as it was to walk into her house that day, it was well worth the risk. I don't know if it brought healing to her life because we didn't connect long enough. I am sure of one thing, she knew I was telling the truth and that all I wanted was for her to find the same hope and assurance that I had received through my messages from Brandy.

I didn't realize it at the time, but I believe something important happened to me that day. I discovered that I had something to give to the world. Brandy's death had been devastating and had turned my world upside down. I would never wish that on another human being, but through it all I had been given an incredible gift. I had a story to tell that could make a difference for others. I could be a messenger of hope to a hurting world. All I needed was an avenue to tell my story.

Chapter 16

He Will Tell the Story

*M*y church is part of a denomination which moves pastors from congregation to congregation. In the first twelve years after Brandy's death I had had three different pastors and a fourth came with his family in July of 2007. Transitions are not always easy for everyone when a family is asked to move. Our new pastor had a twelve-year-old daughter who was not happy about leaving friends from her previous community.

Singing in the church choir has been my gift and a source of great joy. When the new pastor's daughter joined the choir, our director asked me if I would take an interest in her and make her feel welcome. I may have done too good a job as I didn't realize that she was only twelve. She is tall and looks mature for her age so I treated her like an adult. It was not until she shared that her birthday was coming up that I discovered her actual age.

We were practicing for our Easter Cantata when she explained that she expected to receive a cell phone on her next birthday. I asked her when she was born, and she told me March 15. Of course, that date was in my head because it was the day of Brandy's funeral. I probably had a strange look on my face when she added that she was born at 11:00 in the morning. I realized that not only was she born on the day of the funeral, but at the exact moment we were saying goodbye to our daughter. I have come to believe that some things are more than coincidence. Maybe this new pastor and his family had come into my life for a reason.

We have an e-mail ministry in our church that can quickly send out information about prayer concerns or upcoming events. Our new pastor began using the e-mail list to introduce topics in his sermons and invite people to worship. He has a distinctive writing style that I find easily recognizable because he writes just like he talks. I know the e-mail is from him before I ever read his name at the bottom. One afternoon I began reading one of his weekly messages.

> *My sump pump stopped working this week. In many households that is not a big deal, but I am not the most accomplished plumber in the world. I had to go seeking some advice and words of support from a few local experts before I tackled the job of replacing the pump. Soon I headed out to the local hardware store to make my purchase and begin my journey. The*

first thing I discovered was that all the connections from the old sump pump were not the size I needed to connect the new pump. A second trip to Lowes revealed that the exact connections I needed were not always in stock or in the right bin. After 20 minutes of puzzle building, I headed home with what I was 75% sure would work. Miraculously, the pieces all came together, the pump was lowered into the sump (is that the correct term?) and I filled the hole with water. The float went up, the motor started to run and nothing. The water did not empty out of the hole in the ground. I decided to unplug the whole thing before I burned out the motor on my new purchase. Finally I turned to my last resort, I took out the directions. I discovered one little step that I had missed. The directions suggested that I put a hole in the pipe below the floor line to keep the pump from air-locking. It made little sense to put a hole in a pipe that was carrying water, but I didn't have a better plan. Can you believe it actually worked? I plugged the thing back in and water went screaming through the pipe (and out the hole which didn't need to be quite so big). I have officially raised my status to amateur plumber!

What does any of this have to do with worship? I think it is a good metaphor for what I am trying to do with our current sermon series, "When Good

Scriptures Go Bad." For many people, how the church has read some of our scriptures isn't working. Last week was about the environment and this week we will talk about the role of women in the church. What we are trying to do is open up the instruction manual and take a second look. Maybe it is time to drill some holes in the assumptions that have been made about the role of women in the church. I will see you in worship this week.

I laughed as I read the story. I could see him trying to get that sump pump to work and I could feel his frustration. Even more, I could see myself trying to do the same thing. Mechanical things are not my gift. I was home alone reading the story again when I heard a voice as clear as day, "He will tell the story."

I had known for a long time that I was supposed to write this story. Audrey would always say that Brandy wanted her to put everything in writing so that I could remember. I had even tried a few times, but I am simply not a writer. It was not going to happen. Now I had a new option with only one problem. Not only did he not know what I was going to ask, he didn't know the story I was going to ask him to tell.

I decided that I needed my pastor to get to know me before I told him about Brandy. I thought if he could see me as normal then my story would not sound so far out. I invited his family and another couple to come eat at the restaurant after church. All through the meal I could feel Brandy pushing me to talk to him. It was as if she were jabbing her finger into my back, but I couldn't say anything.

After we finished eating, everyone was wandering around the restaurant. There is a lot to look at as each room has a different theme and we have even recreated the old hotel rooms upstairs. My pastor was standing in the gift shop waiting for everyone to finish their self guided tours. I walked up, planning to make a little small talk, but instead just blurted out, "I need to come and talk to you." I don't know what he was thinking I would share, but he calmly replied, "How about this Wednesday."

I have told people my story many times; each time I wonder if the person is going to have an open mind or just think that I am delusional. Most of the time I don't care, but this was my pastor. It was a risk to tell him everything. Some pastors could be very judgmental if my experience did not fit into their theology.

The following Wednesday, I filled a bag to take with me to his office. If he had any questions, I wanted to show him evidence that I was not making this up. At the last minute I decided not to go. I was about to call and cancel when my phone rang. It was my pastor calling to make sure I was still coming. I couldn't say no, so I gathered my bag and my courage and told him I would be there.

I don't think he had any idea what I was coming to share, so I just started from the beginning. I told him whatever came to my mind, not holding anything back. For at least an hour I talked and he listened. I told him that it was not a coincidence that he had come to my church or that his daughter sat next to me in the choir. I apologized for anything I might have said to her that was not appropriate for her age. Finally I shared that I had loved his e-mail about the sump pump, and then I sprang it on him. "I think you are supposed to write the story."

I waited to see how he was going to respond. He had not given me any indication that he thought I was delusional, but I also could not tell if he believed me. Until this time I had not asked him to do anything but listen. Now I was asking him to become part of the story. After what seemed like a long pause but was probably only a few seconds, he said, "My wife is always asking me when I am going to write my first book." He didn't agree to write the book that day, but he didn't say no either.

As I left his office, I called his wife to inform her that I had just laid "a lot of stuff" on her husband. I didn't know what he was thinking, but I didn't mind if he shared it with her. Most of all, I didn't want him to feel obligated to do anything that he didn't want to do. She assured me that if he didn't want to do something, he wouldn't, but if it was a project he felt compelled to work on, then she was confident that it would happen.

What I did not understand is that we couldn't start writing yet because the story was not complete. I had more journeys to take and new people to meet. Brandy was not done communicating; she was about to find a new avenue to send me messages of love and hope. My pastor would be able to decide for himself if my story was real or imagined.

Chapter 17

Was That Clear Enough for You?

Whenever Brandy gave Audrey a song I should listen to or a book I should read, I would go out almost immediately and buy it. The only book I didn't buy was *Many Lives, Many Masters* by Dr. Brian Weiss. Dr. Weiss is a psychiatrist who specializes in past life regressions through hypnosis. Brandy told me through Audrey to read the book but I kept putting it off because I did not believe in reincarnation. I would see the book, on the shelf at bookstores, even pick it up some times, but I would always put it back. I did not want to read it.

One afternoon I was at Wal-Mart buying a card for a friend. I was the only person in the aisle when a book fell off the shelf. I assumed I had knocked it off with my purse, so I picked it up to put it back. When I saw the title, I laughed, it was *Many Lives, Many Masters*. Opening it, I read the front cover before putting it back where it belonged. I had not taken three steps when I heard a sound. The book had fallen off the shelf again. I looked up and said, "I get it, buy the damn book!"

That night I started reading and could not put it down. At three in the morning I took a break and went to look up more information about the author online. I discovered that Dr. Weiss would be speaking in Denver in just two months, so I bought my ticket right then, curious to find out if this man was for real.

The next day I told Tina, one of my employees, what I had done. Tina is one of my best employees, but I would describe her as a hard-living woman. She is very petite but has a mouth like a sailor. I think that is what I love about her. She doesn't pretend to be something she is not. What you see is what you get. She says what she thinks and can be very skeptical. Whenever I told her my stories about Brandy, she just looked at me. She never said she didn't believe me, but I could see the caution in her eyes.

I think Tina wanted to believe me. She had lost two pregnancies so she knew the pain of losing a child. When I told her about my trip to Denver, she asked if anyone was going with me. I told her that Mark had no need to join me, so I was going alone. She thought for a second and then said, "I'll go with you." I was a little surprised, but I didn't mind the company. If she wanted to buy a ticket, I already had a hotel room. She was welcome to come.

The event was held at the Denver Merchandise Mart. I had gone to similar events twice before to see John Edward. The first time I made sure I arrived extra early so I could have a seat in the front row. By now I was veteran and knew it didn't matter where I sat. Besides, I wasn't expecting any messages; I had other priorities for the eight-hour seminar. I wanted to sit where I could see and had easy access to a bathroom.

While everyone else ran for the front rows, we headed to mezzanine where we had our choice of seats. I found two chairs on the end of a row that had a great view of the stage. Eventually a woman from Denver asked if the seat next to us was taken. There were two open chairs so we moved in one to let her sit down. Next a young woman named Kerry asked about the other seat and joined us.

Making small talk, she asked if we were from Colorado. I shared that we had driven all the way from Kansas. She had an interesting accent so I asked her where she lived. Kerry had flown in from Australia, making our eight-hour drive seem like nothing. Casually I commented that she must really be a believer to have come all that way. She responded, "Actually, I do past life regressions." When you attend events like those of Dr. Weiss or John Edward, you learn not to be surprised by the people you meet.

Before I could say anything further, Brian Weiss was introduced and began his presentation. Kerry leaned in, put her hand on my leg and whispered to me, "Your daughter is here."

She gave me a grin and continued, "In fact she wants credit for getting you here." On my other side, Tina was picking up her jaw from the floor. She was stunned by what she was hearing. She had heard my stories for years, but it is very different when you see it for yourself.

Kerry's comment consumed me; I couldn't listen to anything that was happening at the seminar. I didn't want to disrupt Kerry; she had traveled a long way to hear what Dr. Weiss had to say. Still, all I wanted to do was grab this woman and make her tell me everything. Finally the lunch break arrived, and I used the opportunity spend more time with Kerry. I told her my car was nearby and asked her if she would like to join us for lunch. The woman from Denver knew of a Wendy's close to the conference center so the four of us headed out.

Connie, Kerry and Tina at the Brian Weiss Conference

I think everyone who did not purchase a lunch at the seminar decided to eat at Wendy's. The line was huge, and as we waited, I tried to make small talk with my new friend. It was difficult not to blurt out, "Tell me everything my daughter is saying."

I am sure Kerry knew why I had asked her to lunch. As we waited in line she said, "She wants you to tell me about her dog." I thought that was a very odd request. Brandy had had a dog for only ten days, and half of those were spent at the vet. Brandy had wanted a dog badly and promised to take care of it, but she was allergic to dog hair. Some friends of ours found a little black poodle that would not shed. We brought the dog home, but it would not stop coughing. It turned out that the dog was allergic to our carpet.

Kerry insisted that Brandy wanted me to talk about the dog. I asked her if she was sure, but she was certain that there was something about the dog. I told her the story and that Brandy named the dog Popcorn. Kerry stopped me and said, "Now I get it." She explained, "I have a seventeen-year-old daughter who just came home for holiday. She decided she wanted a fish and picked out a little blue fighting fish. Guess what she named it." I knew exactly what she had named it – Popcorn. Kerry explained that she often gets these "out-of-left-field messages" from spirits that appear meaningless to most of us but provide her with validation. It is their way of saying "Hi, it really is me."

After a long wait we bought our food and found a table. I wondered what Tina and our new friend from Denver thought of our conversation, but I had to ask more questions. During our meal, Kerry started touching her neck. She explained, "She is trying to tell me there was choking." Tears began to run down my face. They were a combination of the memory of that night and the reality that she was indeed hearing from my daughter. Kerry continued, "She says to tell you it didn't hurt. She was just so frightened." It was exactly what Audrey had told me years earlier.

By this time I was so emotional that I couldn't speak. Tina was the one who shared the story of how Brandy died. Kerry reassured me, "She is okay now. You will see her again. This separation is only temporary." I thought to myself that she may be okay, but I am definitely not. The pain comes back so easily.

We realized that time was getting away from us, and we needed to go back to the seminar. We quickly made our way back to the conference center and returned to our seats. Dr. Weiss came back onto the stage, but he seemed a little preoccupied. Before he began, he started pacing back and forth, rubbing his hands. After a few moments he shared what was on his mind, "I need to acknowledge that there are parents here who have lost children." I didn't think anything of his comment. I was sure that I was not the only person among the thousands in attendance who had lost a child. He continued, "Your children want you to know that they are with you, the separation is only temporary." That comment seemed an echo of my lunch conversation.

Dr. Weiss continued to pace back and forth, still rubbing his hands as if listening to something. Slowly he said, "Mary... Mary... Mary – the Mother of God." It seemed to come out of nowhere. He paused and then blurted out, "Mary and Medjugorje, I don't know." Then he was done and he began his presentation.

On one side of me Tina was staring with a look of disbelief. I could almost hear the colorful words she wanted desperately to say. On the other side Kerry had a knowing smile on her face and said to me, "Was that clear enough for you!"

Chapter 18

Reconnecting

*W*hen I left Denver, Kerry and I promised to keep in touch. She gave me a card that listed her website, but she warned me that it was still under construction. I checked the site for a couple of weeks, but it was never up and running. Apparently, the construction of the website was taking longer than expected. Eventually I became busy taking care of my dad and running the restaurant and I just stopped looking.

Fourteen months after meeting Kerry in Denver, we were preparing the restaurant for Christmas, when Tina asked if I had looked at her website recently. Tina had run across her card and became curious. She had discovered Kerry's site was no longer under construction. That night I sent Kerry an e-mail through her website. I didn't know if she would remember me, but I decided to take a chance. Within hours I received a response.

A BIG HELLO my friend Connie!

Oh I am so glad you got in touch with me!!! It's a long story, but in short, all my USA & UK trip belongings got put into storage when I arrived back in Australia, as we had to move and they are all still in a box somewhere still in storage. However, that is only a small part of why I am so glad you got in touch and now I have your email – thank you. Yes, I completely remember you both and I was so moved by Brandy coming through for you ... wow it was wonderful and the funny message of confirmation/ validation was the reference of 'Popcorn' – being the same name as a pet – both hers and my daughter's. Do you know I have been doing this ever since I can remember, and I still get blown away by it ... it never ceases to surprise me or get me excited when there is one of those moments that you just go "wow" – coz as you know there is no way that I knew you before hand and of course no way of knowing a "Popcorn" as a pet! I can't recall anything else that came through, so I would love it if you could write me with what you can recall.

I also recall that Brandy... (now I feel really bad about this because at the time it was something I didn't say for Brandy and I hope you understand because of the awkwardness it can make me feel at the time …) but do you remember when you dropped me off at the hotel and just before I was getting out and saying goodbye, Brandy said through me to you "I love you Mom" …

I'm sorry to both you and Brandy, as I stopped myself from saying it as sometimes people can get a bit weird about it. And I said to my husband by phone back to Australia that night, I felt so guilty afterwards for not saying the words to you, from her.

Several weeks after I returned to Australia, my husband and I were driving along and Brandy came through, with a message via a song … it was Madonna singing … a song something about Marlin Brando words in it. It was apparently significant to the timeframe of that song (the 80's or maybe early 90's I think) – this was important to pass on to you. I have no idea what the message is or means, but I'm hoping you will identify with it.

I'm sorry to hear about your father's passing also … he is okay and okay with the world as it is!! That's all I get at the moment, sorry.

I think Brandy has helped push you into making contact with me (as Brandy has just come through now as I am typing) … at last she says …"you were going to connect by email late last year ... what has taken you two so long?" she says (in joking way to stir us both up). I'm going to write out what she is saying ... **the bold type is Brandy** *and the rest is me...*

"Christmas is a special time of year *(she says)* **for both of us"**- *she is smiling*

She is showing me how beautiful she looks in her (and yours) favourite photo – long brownish/tinted hair – curly, and a beautiful smile – stunning!

I see a Christmas tree, all decorated in the corner of the room, and see Brandy as a young child giggling and excited about the tree and decorating it

"I want you to remember the good times, like then" "It was so much fun... and family memories of you and me"

Next . . . and I also see a photo of Brandy wearing a red dress – older now in her teens – not sure if this is the same photo as before – it is more professional style. She is now showing me different casual photos – everywhere on a board, some in the snow like a ski holiday – friends around her in skiing outfits.

I also see her photo being put under the Christmas tree, standing in a frame looking out – not sure if that is what you do, or perhaps it is symbolic of you and Brandy around Christmas time, or maybe she wants you to put her photo under the tree this year – I'm not sure.

She has been worried about you – she has tears – she is showing me that she has kind of taken on the roll of being a mom to you – looking after you from above – guiding you.

"Please no more crying Mom"

"Please tell her I am happy, I want her to lead a happy and fulfilled life, she has so much to give other people, don't let her waste it by worrying so much all of the time." Did you get my message Mom? In the kitchen? *She is showing me... you in the kitchen with winter PJs, dressing gown and slippers – making coffee? Or breakfast? Not sure ... you are thinking and worrying ... you are by yourself ... something about a window in front of kitchen bench/sink ....*

And something about a sofa?

Now we are shopping – she loves shopping... she is having a hard time, or someone is having a hard time working out which one ???

"Go with a splash of color!"

There is a need for you to lean on someone for emotional support – she is showing me a man – it is important it is someone you can trust – he is strong and caring – she wants you to be happy – this emotional support is to come from a male.

Please say hi to Tina for me.

Connie, it was truly beautiful to meet you all (including Brandy) and one of the best reasons… is that Brandy came through for you.

Please stay in touch and thank you again for making contact with me – it is an honour to provide communication for both you and Brandy.

Love to you both
Kerry xoxo

I discovered the Madonna song was called *Vogue* and was recorded in 1990. The first verse says, *Look around everywhere you turn is heartache, It's everywhere that you go, You try everything you can to escape, The pain of life that you know.* I asked Kerry if the person I was leaning on for emotional support was my pastor, and she confirmed that he was the man. The kitchen window is the location of my special Christmas decorations. Finally, I was amazed that she had talked about my sofa. I had just received color samples to have my sofa re-covered. I was planning to go with very plain beige, but Brandy always did have a thing for bright colors.

I mentioned to Kerry that I was taking a trip to Arizona after Christmas, and she wrote back that Brandy wanted me to see a video on Allison Dubois' website. I knew of Allison from her TV show *Medium*, but I had never been compelled to read more about her. I watched the videos on her webpage and found them very interesting. Discovering that Allison had written some books about her life, I decided I needed one for my trip. When I wrote Kerry to share that I had watched the videos and bought a book, she said, "I think there is a chance you can see her in Arizona."

I didn't feel a need to seek out Allison Dubois. I could not imagine her taking the time to see a perfect stranger, so I didn't attempt to contact her. I had received plenty of messages from Audrey and others and now I also had Kerry. What else would Allison Dubois have to tell me? When I returned home from my trip, Kerry sent me another e-mail. It was an advertisement for Allison's speaking tour with a short message: *"Hi Connie - I'm compelled to pass this on to you ... there must be a reason ... any dates on her tour that you can get to?"* I still didn't understand why she was being so persistent. I went online to check her speaking schedule and discovered she would be stopping in Denver. There was no reason to think about it any longer, so I pulled out my credit card and bought a ticket. I decided that I didn't need to be asked again.

Chapter 19

Is This Really Happening to Me?

After all my experiences, you would think that nothing could surprise me anymore. I should just expect the unexpected. Still I went to Denver trying to tell myself that nothing extraordinary would happen. I find it is much easier to keep my expectations low and be pleasantly surprised than to set them too high and be crushed by the results. Besides, I did not need to see Allison Dubois to believe everything that had happened in my life was true. I certainly didn't need her to give me a message from Brandy; I had received those messages. However, it would be dishonest for me to say that I didn't hope all of those things would happen. If Kerry was telling the truth and this was really being orchestrated by Brandy, why wouldn't she make it work?

When my pastor heard I was going to see Allison Dubois, he bought his wife, Diana, a ticket to join me. She is a huge fan of the television show *Medium*. He knew he could score big points by giving her a ticket for her birthday. By now, she had heard all of my stories and could not wait to see what might happen. When we arrived in Denver, we would be joined by Audrey's son Michael who lives in the area.

The night before the event I could not sleep. We were exhausted from our trip, and Diana had no problem closing her eyes. I, on the other hand, was wide awake. I lay in the bed for hours just staring at the ceiling. Finally about 3:00 a.m., I got up to take an Ambien thinking it would knock me out. I checked my phone and there was a message from Kerry. It appeared that I was not the only person was being kept awake.

> *Wow – what a noisy bunch of guys you have on the other side Connie!! I had them all in my bedroom last night – really excited – totally noisy and chatting amongst themselves – essentially having a party in my bedroom!!! All in anticipation for the event coming up over there!!! This was from around 1:00 a.m. thru to about 2:00 a.m. or so. I had to tell them to leave and go back over there. I think it was around your lunch time over there as I could see you having lunch together – could smell hot food and could hear crockery and glass – more on that later.*

This Scottish dude came through first – quite jovial and had a really good sense of humour about his role … he said in his gorgeous accent … "this lassie (Allison) is quite the fayreground attraction eh…. Listen to the crowd coming (from the other side with him) …. I'm doing my best to control the crowd" …. He smiled and then got me to hear the crowds of people on the other side – wow what a noise!!!! If you can imagine the number of people (living) getting ready to attend the event later that day - then triple it, it is the sound of a sports event on steroids!!! So can you imagine just how many souls there are . . . all wanting to watch or be heard when Allison is the conductor of the show?

Anyhow, then your crowd walks into my bedroom…. Whoa – what a noise – funny though!! But they had no real idea that they were in an apartment in Brisbane, Australia, interrupting me getting to sleep though – they were quite oblivious to where they were. Hilarious!! Miss B was actually quiet and just observing!! Scottish dude had a sense of humour – I think he was showing me what he had to deal with in regards to this role he had to play – just wanted to share it with me. I seriously couldn't get over the noise – chatters, laughter and funny ways of talking over the top of each other … anyhow I ended up getting them to move out and on back to where they should be – with you!!

Anyhow must go – Catherine and I are having time together this arvo to get our nails done and then I am back in the office later today.

Look forward to hearing all about the event – God I hope someone in your group got a reading or something eventful happened – for you to go all that way – and not to mention me not getting any sleep because of your noisy crowd!! What a hoot they were!!

> *Big hugs and smiles*
> *Kerry*

The next day we headed to the convention center hours early. I am a bit of a freak when it comes to being late so I didn't want to take any chances. We met Michael, found the place we were going and then shared a late lunch together in an open air mall. We had plenty of time to talk as my anxiety about being late had given us about a three-hour cushion.

Our tickets included a VIP Meet-and-Greet before the event, so about 5:30 we headed into the convention center. I was surprised that it was not a bigger venue. The room seated only around 300 people, and only forty had purchased the VIP tickets. Allison sat at a small table to meet people and sign books. In our excitement to get there, I realized that we had not brought anything to have her sign. We had left all of her books at home. I didn't even have a paper and pencil. We found our seats on the second row and then waited our turn in line to talk to her.

I have never been accused of having nothing to say. Nearly every day I say something that makes me wonder when I will learn to keep my mouth shut. As we stood in line, I began to get this big lump in my throat and the tears started to flow. Michael put his arm around me to calm me, but as I stepped up to talk to Allison I was practically speechless. The only words I could get to come out of my mouth were "Thank you… Thank you for what you do." I felt like such a dope.

Graciously, Allison complimented the color of my sweater and thanked me for understanding how difficult it is to do what she does, saying not everyone appreciates her gifts. No matter how many times she tries to prove that her messages are authentic and genuine, there are always critics who want just a little more evidence.

We sat back down, and a little before 7:00 the rest of the public entered into the room. Allison had a cousin who was acting as host. He introduced Allison and then explained what to expect from the evening. The first hour would be life questions. Members of the audience could ask questions about careers, relationships, projects or any other matters that were on their mind. Allison would not be connecting to specific people, but she would share insights into their lives. In the second hour she would connect to loved ones who had passed.

There were many hands that went up in the room, but not many could be answered because Allison took 10-15 minutes addressing each question. The second person she called on was my pastor's wife. Diana asked for validation of a project her husband was working on that was outside of his career. Allison said she needed to be a little more specific, so Diana told her that he was working on a book. Allison's response was gentle and caring. She talked about the couples' relationship, how he was the dreamer and she was the anchor. She shared how blessed they were, and then she said, "The book will not do what he expects." I took that to mean that we are wasting our time writing this story. Michael and Diana understood it entirely differently. They knew that my pastor was helping me to write this with absolutely no expectations.

Because Allison had spoken to Diana, I was sure that I had no chance. There were hundreds of people who had come hoping to hear a word from someone they loved. It was selfish for me to want a message from Brandy when I had already received that gift many times. Really I was protecting myself from disappointment. I needed to raise my defenses by lowering any expectations that were sitting in the back of my mind. I started to question why I had come all this way in the first place. Was it just to hear that the book would not do what we expected? We didn't need Allison to tell us that.

During the last hour, Allison brought audience members to the stage for readings. A little before 9:00 I looked down at my watch and realized she was on her last person. Michael got up from his seat, I assumed to make a trip to the restroom. Just after 9:00 he sat back down and I reached over and patted him on his leg. He had not been to the restroom after all. Something had instructed him to get up and change the energy in the room. If I was to get a reading, then he needed to move. Michael stood in the foyer until the same voice told him that he could return to his seat.

Allison finished her reading and stood up to give her closing remarks. Before she could say anything, the host interrupted her and said he thought she needed to speak with one more. Allison didn't argue; she simply sat back down. He looked directly in my eyes and invited me onstage. I was now caught speechless for the second time in one night.

As I sat in one of the armchairs on stage, Allison asked my name and who I wanted to hear from. On a yellow legal pad, Allison wrote my name and the word daughter and then began to scribble on the pad. She wrote the entire time she was talking about Brandy.

Brandy was an absolute hoot. Allison started by telling me that Brandy believed she was probably the smartest person I knew. That was an inside joke because she was smart, but she was also just about the biggest ditz I ever knew and I never hesitated to tell her. Allison shared that Brandy had long blond hair and that she was good at everything. I had to speak up and remind her that she was not good at everything; in fact, she was horrible at tennis. She did, however, look very cute in her tennis outfit. This got a laugh from the audience but Allison reminded me that I was not there to nitpick.

My friends said I appeared stunned the entire time I sat on the stage. Fortunately, they were writing things down as fast as they could because much of the experience is blurred in my mind. Allison continued to share details about Brandy that were incredibly accurate. She talked about how she loves the holidays and about the hundreds of people that came to her funeral. She spoke of her love for dancing and of seeing a picture of Brandy when she was five, wearing dance shoes, a leotard and fairy wings. She told me things that I had forgotten such as how her high school friends had raised money to put a picture of her in the school library.

Allison shared things that I heard many times from Audrey. She said that Brandy was a very strong energy and that she was surrounded by a bright light. She reminded me that Brandy is able to reach me through music and that Brandy is surrounded by children, but maybe the most important thing she told me is that I blame myself for everything. However, Brandy wants me to know that her death was not my fault. I do not need to take responsibility for her death and neither does Brandy. I need to let it go so that I can find healing. Then Allison said something that sent chills down my spine: "Remember she chose you to be her mother. Do not forget that; she chose you and she will always be with you."

I was in tears again, overwhelmed by what was happening. Maybe that is why I said something really stupid. I told Allison that I really hadn't needed this and that I didn't want to come to Denver. Realizing how ungrateful I sounded, I tried to explain that what I had said had come out all wrong. What I meant is that I already knew everything she told me. I have been blessed with other people in my life that can connect with Brandy. I think I was feeling guilty for all the others who came to see Allison hoping to get a reading. Why was this happening to me again?

I don't remember how I got off stage, but as I sat back down in my chair, I was surrounded by people in the room who wanted to talk. They were writing down their e-mails addresses and phone numbers to share with me. I am very fortunate that Michael and Diana were there to collect everything for me because I was still shaking from what I had just received. I want to say that I did not need to hear from Brandy through Allison, but that is not true. When a parent loses a child, the only thing you want in life is to hear from that person one more time. You live for that connection and it can never be enough. I have no doubt that I was led to see Allison just as I was led to every other connection I have made to Brandy in my life, but this time I realized that it was not just for me. As people started coming to talk after the event, I knew that I could be part of their healing. They needed someone to give them hope. My story could offer hope that they too will connect with their loved ones who have passed from this life.

I have a great fear about what others will think if I tell them what has happened. I don't want to be judged as that crazy lady who talks to her dead daughter. I know what it is like to have people doubt my story. My trip to see Allison was the final step in overcoming that fear. She reminded me that people will always judge you for something; sometimes it is as shallow as how your hair looks or the clothes you are wearing. You cannot live your life in fear of being judged. On the other hand, taking a risk and telling my story has great possibilities for bringing healing to many people who are hurting. I have a great opportunity to share not only what has happened but what I have learned. It is time to put on my big girl pants and use the most painful event in my life to make a difference.

Chapter 20

Why Questions

In the fifteen years since Brandy's death I have asked a lot of questions; most of them begin with why? Why did Brandy have to die? Why did we not take her back to the hospital? Why did Brandy make contact with Audrey and others? Why do so many others never hear back from their loved ones? Why am I writing all of this?

The events that have taken place have caused me to think about matters that I had never before considered. Until her death I had sailed through life with few problems or pain. Questions of faith and what comes after this life were not on my radar. It was so easy to take things for granted when they were going well, but it was in those times of deepest despair that I realized we can't always handle things alone and that control is just an illusion. One thing is very clear. No amount of money or wishing can undo the pain or bring my precious child home to me.

One of the gifts I have received is that I no longer fear death. Before Brandy's death, there was nobody more afraid of dying. I didn't even want to talk about it. My mother tried to prepare me for the time when she would be gone by showing me where to find important documents. I refused. I wanted to live in denial. She would say to me, "Connie, you may not want to talk about this, but it is part of life. That is just the way it is. Death is a part of living. I know you don't want to face it, but you have to."

I have learned that death is not the end but a transition to a new life. The experiences of the past fifteen years have made it much easier to let both of my parents go. I still miss them every day, but I also live with a confidence that they are not really gone and that I will see them again. That confidence gives me a sense of comfort. I wonder how people who don't believe in an afterlife cope with the loss of the people they love. Where do they find comfort and hope?

After Brandy died, I asked Audrey where she went. Where do our loved ones go when they die? Her answer was that they are all around us. They are very aware of our lives and surround us with their love. Brandy told her that we are so close that if I could unzip the air and stick my hand through, I would feel her. We will always be together.

A mural we had painted at the Brookville Hotel called
Brandy's Opera House

When Brandy died, our neighbors who lived across the street were in Europe. After they returned, she brought a card over to my house. The card was incredibly meaningful so I asked her where it came from. She was hesitant, but she finally told me the story. She and her husband were in a cathedral in England looking at some prayer cards for sale in a gift shop when she heard Brandy's voice say, "Will you get that for my mother?" She thought it was strange, not only because Brandy was not in England but she had no knowledge of her death. She bought the card anyway and later called home to discover what had happened. As I look back now, the words on the card carry even greater meaning.

> *"Death is nothing at all. I have only slipped away into*
> *the next room. I am I, and you are you. Whatever*
> *we were to each other, that we still are. Call me*
> *by my old familiar name, speak to me in the easy*

way which you always used. Put no difference in your tone, wear no forced air of solemnity or sorrow. Laugh as we always laughed at the little jokes we enjoyed together. Play, smile, think of me, pray for me. Let my name be ever the household word that it always was, let it be spoken without effort, without the trace of a shadow on it. Life means all that it ever meant. It is the same as it ever was; there is unbroken continuity. Why should I be out of mind because I am out of sight? I am waiting for you, for an interval, somewhere very near, just round the corner. All is well."

- Henry Scott Holland

One of my why questions is why I cannot hear messages from Brandy like Audrey and Kerry. Why do I have to rely on others to communicate with my daughter? Why do I have to trust that they are telling me the truth? One reason is that if she did ever appear to me, I would never be able to let her go. Brandy once told Audrey that she would not come back even if she could. I was offended by the message. Why would she not want to come back to be with her mother? Her response was if I only understood the glory of where she was, I wouldn't ask her to come back. I don't think she knows how desperate I am to have her in my life.

On one occasion I was fortunate enough to experience her in a dream. I normally don't remember my dreams, but this one was intensely vivid. It was after my father died, but I dreamed that I was walking down the hall toward his room in the retirement home. I had taken that trip many times, and I dreaded it because I never knew what I was going to find when I reached his door. Would he be in his right mind; would he even recognize me? Walking down the hall I passed my cousin who is very much alive. She stopped and said to me, "They're all here."

Opening the door to my father's room, I discovered that it was not his room at all. Inside was a grand piano and my mother was playing while my sister stood behind her singing. That is what my family did for entertainment. We gathered around the piano while my mother played and we sang songs. As I entered the room, I knew that I was asleep and that these people had all died. I walked over to my mother and hugged her. I was surprised at how cold she was. She never stopped playing, but she turned her head and kissed me. I asked her where Daddy was and she pointed to the corner. I looked to see him waving at me as he always did with his hand right next to his eye. I asked if Brandy was there, and Kristie pointed to her across the room. She waved at me, but didn't come over. The next thing I knew, I was awake.

I couldn't keep this to myself so I woke Mark up. Tears were flowing down my cheeks as I said, "I just saw them all." I told Mark the story of my dream. He responded, "Wow! I think you just received a gift." He was right. I was disappointed that I had woken from the dream. I wanted desperately to go back to the room and spend time with my family again.

If all these things had not happened to me, I would not have believed them. I don't know how many times I have asked myself if they really happened or if I am just making them up out of some need to believe or cope. When I have these thoughts, a good friend of mine often asks, "Connie, how many times do these things have to happen before you will believe." My answer always seems to be, "Just one more!"

Audrey has been a courageous friend to be the medium for the message. She never asked to be part of this journey and I know it has not been easy for her. She was generous to ask Brandy all of my questions and write down answers, even when it was difficult or more convenient to call on the phone. In her journal she wrote the following message from Brandy that tries to answer the question of why.

> *Each living creature and thing God has made is given something, a burden to bear while we are here on this earth. Some are similar, some are very different. Each person finds that how they feel and how they handle it is totally up to them. For some it is a living hell here on earth, for others it is a welcomed gift. To each one of us it is our unique life experience. We can be angry and full of hate or we can totally surrender to God and ask for His help.*
>
> *We can give up and totally consume our life in ourselves or we can each lift our head up to Him and continue on this journey, accept what happens and know that someday our life will end in total happiness. We are all here together to help each other on this journey with love and compassion and understanding, not to judge one another and think our life is worse, but to help each other for no other*

reason but love. If we ask why, we will get no answer – if we ask for total understanding, we will get no answer. If we ask for help, it is there.

Once we realize that we are not in total control and resign ourselves to the fact that we cannot live without His love, we then will have more understanding of the events that happen in our life and resign ourselves to go on and continue this journey of total love and surrender. It is then that we will find happiness here on this earth – each different – each in our own unique way.

I love you mother and daddy and I am there to help you on this journey, welcome it. We will be together again.

Love,
Brandy

Chapter 21

Love Never Ends

I have asked myself many times why my story has had such a deep connection to the Catholic Church. It is not a Catholic story and I come from a strong Protestant background. I have a friend who is sure that I have missed the point because I have not converted to Catholicism. She is convinced that a dark entity is after my soul and that my only hope is to join the Catholic Church. Other friends have the opposite concerns. They struggle with many of the teachings found in Catholicism and are afraid that I will convert.

I have a great appreciation for the Catholic Church and I have been blessed because of the church and my many friends who are Catholic. There are many cathedrals I have entered and immediately felt the presence of God. I have participated in the

Mass and many of the rituals of the church. I light a candle for Brandy every chance I get, but I do not intend to convert to Catholicism. I don't believe it is necessary or that God is leading me in that direction. I am sure that is a great relief to some of my friends and a disappointment to others.

Even though my spirit is fed by the Christian faith, I am not so arrogant to believe that it is the only path that leads to God. I believe that God's greatest desire is to love us unconditionally and to pull us back to that source of love that created us in the first place. Life is not some game where we have to pick the right religious tradition if we want to win the prize. I believe there is truth and wisdom in every religion and that God will use any means possible to guide us back to love. That does not mean that I think all religions are the same. There are great differences in each tradition; there are even vast disagreements within religions. What I am trying to say is that the paths may be different, but God's desire is that each will take us back to our source which is rooted in love.

From the beginning Mary has been an important piece of the story. Audrey told me many times that Brandy is working with Mary. She is taking care of the children who are lost and have no parents. Whenever I hear stories of children who have been orphaned because of AIDS or war, my heart breaks and I feel compelled to act. A few years ago my church hosted an African Children's Choir from Uganda. The children were so beautiful and had such an energetic spirit that the entire church was moved. When I heard their story, that each child had lost one or both parents, I could feel Brandy whispering in my ear, "These are the children I love. You must love them too." I went home and told Mark I was going to make substantial donation and he needed to get out his check book and match it.

I think one of the reasons that Mary is so important to our story is that she knows what it is like to watch her child die. I can relate to her story and she can relate to mine. Unless you have lost a child to death, you cannot understand the pain. It is deeper than words can explain. In the Gospel of Luke there is a story of Mary and Joseph taking the baby Jesus to Jerusalem where they meet a man named Simeon. Simeon takes the child in his arms and praises God that he has had the opportunity to witness the salvation contained in this child. He then turns to Mary and tells her that rearing this child will not be easy; not everyone will be as excited to see Jesus as he has been. He then says the line that captures my pain, "and a sword will pierce your own soul too." The day Brandy died my soul was pierced in a way that only Mary could understand.

That is why I was so drawn to the picture of Mary that hangs in our restaurant, the same picture that caught the attention of the doctor who visited and encouraged me to tell the story. He said, "You will bring many to her Son through your sorrows." I know that is true because I have seen it happen. Not everyone is going to connect to my story. Some will try to dismiss it as fantasy or delusion, but others will be given comfort and find themselves drawn into the love that is embodied and revealed through Jesus. I do not claim that Jesus is the only way to God, but Jesus has been the most important story in my life. It is the story of a God who loves the world so much that He would do anything, even become one of us if that would convey his love for us. In the story of Jesus found in the Gospels, God does not choose to go to the wealthy and powerful, but to those who hurt the most: the least, the last and the lost. God says to them, "You are not alone."

When Brandy died, I was lost in my pain. I no longer wanted to live. There was no reason to continue, but I was saved by love. It was through the love of friends, the love of my daughter and ultimately the love of God that I began to heal. I discovered that the Apostle Paul was correct when he claimed the greatest power in life is love; without it we are nothing. And here is the best news of all – love never ends. Even death cannot stop the power of love. That is the story of Jesus and that is what I discovered in my own story.

As I come to the end of this book, I realize that there is no end because love has no end. Brandy will continue to be part of my life until that day I see her again on the other side. I have tried to share many of the things that have happened to me since Brandy's death. So many wonderful things have happened to me over the past fifteen years. I have been blessed with friends who have walked with me on this journey. They have listened to my stories without judgment and are still my friends. They have showed me more patience than I deserved as I have found healing and hope.

I suppose the most important thing I have learned from all of this is that we are not alone. We are surrounded by God's love. We just have to open our eyes and embrace it. God's love is lived out through friends who walk with us in the good times and the bad. God's love remains present in our lives through the people that have passed over to the other side but remain connected to our lives here on earth. Finally, God's love flows through us as we reach out to one another through acts of kindness and grace. We are called to be agents of God's love in the world.

It would have been so much easier never to write this book. I have worried many times what people will think about me and even more how this will affect those who have been part of my story. It is our human nature to criticize that which we don't understand. I know because I do it just like everyone else. It is difficult to open our minds to something that does not fit in our box. It would have been easier not to write, but God doesn't ask us to do what is easy. God asks us to love unconditionally just as he loves us. This book is my act of love. It is my attempt to share the love that I have found with people who have experienced the pain of loss. It is my hope that through my actions, others will discover the power of love.

Chapter 22

The Final Word

There is no end to this story but there is a final word – Love. The very first words that Brandy gave to Audrey were of love. She made sure that love was the most important thing. Love is the only solution to the incredible pain in our world. We can find healing in love, but we also have a responsibility to share that love with others.

I hope that I have been changed by these events in my life. I like to believe that I am less judgmental and more willing to love, but I know that I am still working on that one. I am far from perfect and I have much more to learn. I am trying every day to be more accepting and loving to the people in my life. There are so many things that we do to one another that get in the way of love. Will we ever learn how important it is to love?

The biggest question I face is why all of this has happened to me. Why have I received this incredible gift from Brandy? Mothers lose children every day and don't have the same experiences. Their pain is as great as mine yet they are still waiting for a word of assurance. I don't have an answer to why, but maybe that is the wrong question. The real question is what can I do in response to this gift? How can I share the message of love that I have received? What I can do is have the courage to share my story with the desire that someone else may discover comfort and hope through the power of love. Early on in my journey, Brandy sent me a message through Audrey that seems more relevant today.

> God has breathed new life into you mother, it is your new beginning. Your life is important, there is so much you must do now. He has given you this help so that you can go and help others. They will come and you will help them. Some of the days to come will be very difficult. You must remember to only ask God for the help and he will give it to you. He is within you now, showing you the way. Remember this always. You are blest.
>
> I am so proud of you. You have come so far. Please tell Daddy I love him so very much. I love you both so very much. We always will be a family, a family of love within God. I am with you both always and I pray that you will hear me some day.
>
> God has truly blessed us all, our entire family. Help them all Mother — you must be the strong one now. God is within us, all of our senses, our very being, the purpose of our lives. He loves us so

much and we must share this love with others. You will spread the seeds and the beautiful flowers will grow to show Him our love. Please, please, I beg you Mother, remember all of these things. I am with you always. Don't despair, life is so beautiful, embrace it. People will know that through you, God is with us all. Raise your beautiful voice and sing praises to Him. Share your life with everyone that needs you. He loves you so much; He has given you so much, now you must return His love.

Your life has a purpose. As you breathe each day and smell the earth, the flowers, the creatures of this earth, spring will come again to remind you of the new life that God has given you. I am there within it all. The music will continue. I will continue to help you. Don't give up, I will be there. God loves us all.

Please try to understand and help Daddy. He also needs to feel my love and know that I am with him. His life also has a purpose. I want him to know that I was going to come back and help him with the restaurant. Please don't leave it. It will always be like home to me filled with so many memories of our lives. Continue at night, I see the people come, the lights of the hotel burning, the smell, the laughter – I love it. I am there.

I love you both always. I am there with you.

Love,
Brandy

CPSIA information can be obtained
at www.ICGtesting.com
Printed in the USA
FFOW04n1457311214
9988FF